Cornelia "recites" for Monsieur de la Croix. The Catholic University Theatre production.

Our Hearts Were Young and Gay

DRAMATIZED BY

JEAN KERR

FROM THE BOOK BY
CORNELIA OTIS SKINNER AND
EMILY KIMBROUGH

THE DRAMATIC PUBLISHING COMPANY
CHICAGO

Notice

THE attention of all purchasers is directed to the following: This work is fully protected under the copyright laws. Violations of the Copyright Law are punishable by fine or imprisonment, or both.

The royalty fee for one performance of this play by amateurs is **twenty-five dollars ($25.00)**. Arrangements must be made in advance of the performance. Royalty of the required amount must be paid whether the play is presented for charity or gain and whether admission is charged or not. Since performance of this play without permission renders anybody participating liable to severe penalties imposed by law, anybody acting in this play, or participating in any way in its performance, should be sure, before doing so, that the necessary permission has been obtained.

No radio broadcast of this play may be made.

Copyright covers, among other rights, the right to make copies; and the copying by hand, by typewriter, or by any other process, of "parts" or of any portion of a copyrighted play is dishonest and illegal, and, since it is an infringement of the copyright, will be vigorously prosecuted.

On all programs and advertising this notice must appear: Produced by special arrangement with THE DRAMATIC PUBLISHING COMPANY, of Chicago.

Our Hearts Were Young and Gay

A Comedy in Three Acts

FOR EIGHT MEN AND NINE WOMEN

"Our Hearts Were Young and Gay" was given its première production by the Speech and Drama Department of The Catholic University, Washington, D. C., under the direction of Walter Kerr, with settings and lighting by Ruth Shimigelsky. The cast was as follows:

(In the order of their appearance)

STEWARD .... Anthony Brink
MRS. SKINNER .... Eileen Whyte
CORNELIA OTIS SKINNER .... Jacqueline Hastings
OTIS SKINNER .... John McGiver
EMILY KIMBROUGH .... Hyacinth Larkin
PURSER .... Dan Rodden
STEWARDESS .... Evelyn Schneider
DICK WINTERS .... Albert Martin
ADMIRAL .... John Easely
HARRIET ST. JOHN .... Alice Dunbar
WINIFRED BLAUGH .... Florence Ffrench
LEO McEVOY .... Bill McGuire
INSPECTOR .... Dorothy Chernuck
THÉRÈSE .... Angelita Reynosa
MADAME ELISE .... Dorothy Lynch
MONSIEUR DE LA CROIX .... Aime Grandmaison
WINDOW CLEANER .... Dan Rodden

THE SCENES

ACT ONE: *A cabin, aboard ship. Summer. The year, 1923.*

ACT TWO, *Scene One: The same. About ten days later. Late evening.*

   Scene Two: The same. Early next morning.

ACT THREE, *Scene One: A small hotel in Paris. Two weeks later.*

   Scene Two: The same. Eleven o'clock, the next morning.

   Scene Three: The same. About a month later.

NOTE: The Window Cleaner (Act III) can be doubled with one of the men on shipboard (Admiral, Purser, or Steward), reducing the number of men to seven.

GENERAL PRODUCTION NOTE

The play is devised to be done in one (unit) set, if desired. This means that the same essential flats in the same arrangement can be used for both scenes, with different properties blocking out certain features alternately to give an effect of change. In this manner:

The bunk beds in the cabin, with the aid of some drapes, cover up the two windows, which are then not seen at all until the hotel sequences.

The bathroom door in the cabin is blocked off by a hanging tapestry in the hotel arrangement, with the telephone stand against it.

The cabinet arrangement in the cabin becomes the full door to the bathroom in the hotel. Pictures cover the portholes on this wall.

The center door remains the same, although a rehinging of different actual doors into the door frame will help. The cabin door, then, would be painted to give an effect of steel, the hotel door of wood. The corridor backings beyond are to be changed, adding to the difference of effect.

The use of entirely new properties, of different character, and arranged very differently, will, of course, assist in varying the impression.

Further production notes, on costumes, properties, etc., will be found at the end of the play.

ACT ONE

SCENE: *The interior of a cabin, aboard ship. The year, 1923. The entrance from the corridor is upstage center, with a very narrow corridor backing beyond it. A door down left leads to the bathroom. Just above this door are double-deck bunks for sleeping, against the wall. In the middle of the right wall is either a full door, or, if possible, a cabinet-effect opening which conceals a washbasin. Below this, at right stage, stands a small table. In the right wall, on either side of the cabinet-effect, are portholes. There is a wicker chaise lounge right of center, and a hassock down center.*]

AT RISE OF CURTAIN: *The cabin is empty. Whistles are heard offstage, and the normal banging and clanging of a ship's loading. Band music is heard somewhere in the distance. Aside from some remote shouting, there are now sounds of voices in the corridor outside, and the door up center is opened by the* STEWARD, *who steps in smartly, speaking back into the corridor.*]

STEWARD. Cabin for Miss Skinner and Miss Kimbrough. This way, please.

[MRS. SKINNER, *Cornelia's mother, appears in the doorway, up center, calling back.*]

MRS. SKINNER. Cornelia! Here it is! You don't have to look in all the cabins, dear. We've found it!

[MRS. SKINNER *heads for the table and deposits her purse and a package, as* CORNELIA *appears in the doorway, up center, wide-eyed and silent.*]

7

MRS. SKINNER. Now, Steward, you'll show Miss Skinner where everything is, won't you?

STEWARD. Yes, ma'am.

MRS. SKINNER. Cornelia, dear, make sure you understand everything!

STEWARD [*going to the door, down left, as* CORNELIA *tries to concentrate*]. This is the bath, miss.

MRS. SKINNER. Cornelia! Do you hear? That's the bath.

[MRS. SKINNER *tries the door herself, to make sure* CORNELIA *grasps it, as the* STEWARD *crosses to right stage.* CORNELIA *nods, automatically.*]

MRS. SKINNER. Oh, and here are your beds! Bunks, they call them, dear. So seaman-like! I wonder if you ought to sleep up—and Emily down, or Emily up and you down?

STEWARD [*as* CORNELIA *turns from one to the other, trying to grasp instructions*]. You'll find the washbasin here, miss.

[*The* STEWARD *opens the cabinet and shuts it.* CORNELIA *continues to nod, vacantly.*]

MRS. SKINNER. See, Cornelia? That's the washbasin. [*She tests the bunks with her hands.*] I *do* wonder about these beds—[*She speaks over her shoulder.*]—Cornelia, who weighs most—you or Emily? [*She continues before* CORNELIA *can reply.*] I suppose you do, dear. Although I must say you've been looking very trim lately. It's nice to see you losing that baby fat.

CORNELIA [*embarrassed before the* STEWARD]. Mother! . . .

STEWARD [*quickly pointing to the button on the wall by the up center door*]. Just ring this if you wish anything, miss.

MRS. SKINNER. Now, where's your father? Cornelia, we've lost your father! [*She calls out the door, up center.*] Otis! Otis! Here we are!

STEWARD. May I have the tags for your trunks, miss?

CORNELIA. Oh, yes.

[*Hurriedly and awkwardly*, CORNELIA *dives into her purse, bringing out the tags.* OTIS SKINNER, CORNELIA'S *father, appears in the doorway, up center, hot and puffing slightly.*]

MRS. SKINNER. Otis, you *must* keep up with us! We've only got a few moments to say good-bye to our baby——

CORNELIA [*anguished*]. Mother! . . .

OTIS. Keep up with you! One more flight of stairs down and I'd have had a heart attack. [*He flops onto the end of the chaise lounge.*]

MRS. SKINNER. You've only yourself to thank. When you said you wanted to see the cabin, Cornelia *told* you it was below deck.

OTIS. What she neglected to mention was that it was so far down that it's actually resting on the keel!

STEWARD [*having put everything to rights*]. I'll see to the trunks immediately, miss. Will there be anything else?

CORNELIA [*anxious to be rid of the* STEWARD]. No. No, thank you. That's—all.

[*The* STEWARD *remains standing, expectantly.* CORNELIA *turns to* MRS. SKINNER, *vaguely.*]

CORNELIA. That *is* all, Mother, isn't it?

MRS. SKINNER. Cornelia, dear! . . .

[MRS. SKINNER *makes an elaborate silent motion to* CORNELIA'S *purse and the* STEWARD, *so that he cannot miss it. The* STEWARD *pretends to look away.*]

OTIS [*bellowing*]. Tip the man, Cornelia! He's in business.

CORNELIA [*blushing*]. Father!

[CORNELIA *hastily dives into her purse again and gives the* STEWARD *some change.*]

STEWARD. Thank you, miss. Which of the trunks do you want brought to the cabin, miss?

CORNELIA. Oh—all of them, of course.

MRS. SKINNER. Cornelia! You won't want them all just for the two weeks on shipboard!

CORNELIA [*firmly, with great patience*]. Mother! How would you know? My crepe dress is in one trunk, and the shoes that go with it in another, and——

OTIS [*with a flourish to end it*]. *All* the trunks, Steward. Ship ahoy!

STEWARD [*with a slightly peculiar look, but obediently going to the door*]. Yes, sir. Yes, miss. Right away, miss.

[*The* STEWARD *goes out, up center, shutting the door behind him.*]

MRS. SKINNER. Now, Otis, you can't sit there! Our own boat goes before Cornelia's does, you know——

CORNELIA [*who has opened the door to make sure the* STEWARD *is out of earshot, closing it, and turning to* OTIS *and* MRS. SKINNER]. Mother! Why did you have to humiliate me?

MRS. SKINNER. Humiliate you?

CORNELIA. Yes, exactly! Here I am, going on an ocean voyage with that man——[*She points to the door the Steward has used.*]

OTIS. You're *what?*

CORNELIA. —who doesn't know anything about me, and here you are, right off, giving him the impression I'm a *baby!*

MRS. SKINNER. Well, after all, Cornelia, you're only nineteen! [*She suddenly turns to* OTIS.] Oh, Otis! Do you think we should let her do it?

OTIS. *I* don't see any sense in it.

[CORNELIA'S *eyes go to the heavens as "this" starts all over again.*]

OTIS. Here we are! You and I going to Paris—and Cornelia and Emily going to Paris. On two different boats! *What for?* There's room on our boat! It's not a canoe!

CORNELIA [*exasperated, throwing off her hat and going to* OTIS, *despairingly*]. But, Father! That's the whole point of this trip! Emily and I are growing up! Maturing! You might say that we were becoming emancipated.

OTIS. Yes, you *might*. I wouldn't, but you might.

CORNELIA [*with the patient exasperation of a child for its elders*]. Father, it's my money. I saved it up. Emily saved up hers, too.

OTIS. Well, they take money on our boat. They're taking *mine!*

CORNELIA. But it's more expensive! This may not be very stylish, but don't you see? It's all our own!

OTIS. Great Scott! You haven't *bought* the blasted thing, have you?

CORNELIA. You know perfectly well what I mean. We'll be independent. After all, I can't always be a leech, sucking away at your vitals.

OTIS [*to* MRS. SKINNER, *dramatically*]. Maud! Does this child *have* to talk like that?

MRS. SKINNER. Cornelia, dear, don't be so dramatic. [*She goes about her business.*] I'll turn down your beds for you.

OTIS. You'll be lucky if this old tub gets out the harbor. *I* know what it reminds me of! The tomb scene! [*Having fun for himself, he declaims.*]

"Shall we stay in this palace of dim night?

Alack, what blood is this which stains the stony entrance of this sepulchre?

[*He extends his hand to* CORNELIA.]

Lady, come away from this nest of death, contagion, and unnatural sleep."

[CORNELIA *pulls her hand back, starting to laugh in spite of herself.*]

MRS. SKINNER. Otis, we haven't time for "Romeo and Juliet."

CORNELIA. Besides, Father, I have to save extra for the lessons! As soon as we get to Paris, I'm going to take acting lessons from Monsieur de la Croix at the Comédie Française, if he'll take me.

MRS. SKINNER [*worried*]. Dear, I don't like you consorting with strange Frenchmen. Couldn't you have taken lessons from an American actor?

CORNELIA. Mother! There's no one in the American theatre today. Simply no one!

[OTIS *raises a magnificent eyebrow.*]

CORNELIA. Oh, Father! I don't count *you!* Besides, I know all your tricks.

OTIS [*thundering, to* MRS. SKINNER, *and enjoying himself*]. Tricks!

[*The* STEWARD *opens the door, up center, smartly.*]

STEWARD. All ashore that's going ashore!

[*The* STEWARD *closes the door, and disappears.*]

MRS. SKINNER [*looking at her watch*]. Oh, *dear*, I can't bear to think of leaving you until Emily gets here—but we've got our own boat to catch!

OTIS. Yes. I don't feel up to rowing across.

CORNELIA [*relieved now and very gay*]. I can hardly wait to see Emily. I've missed her so desperately.

OTIS. How long is it since you've seen her?

CORNELIA. Not since school closed, Father. Ten days ago!

OTIS. Well, I hope you won't find her too much changed.

MRS. SKINNER. Cornelia, dear. Before we go, there are a few things I must say to you.

[CORNELIA *becomes obedient and a little grave.*]

OTIS. I'll bet Emily's already on board and got lost in that labyrinth out there. [*He goes to the door, up center.*] E-mily! E-mily!

CORNELIA. Yes, Mother?

MRS. SKINNER. Whatever you do, dear, you must not talk to strange men.

[OTIS *snorts in the doorway.*]

MRS. SKINNER. And do stand up straight and keep your shoulders back—so you'll look pretty.

OTIS. So strange men will talk to her.

MRS. SKINNER [*with a hushing glance at* OTIS]. Don't be trying out your acting all the time, dear. Just when the occasion calls for it, like a ship's concert or something. Or better still, save it for that Monsieur Whatever-his-name is. I *do* hope he's a gentleman.

CORNELIA. Yes, Mother.

MRS. SKINNER. And, oh, yes! I have a little present for you.

CORNELIA [*surprised*]. You have?

MRS. SKINNER [*having taken the package from the table, where she put it earlier*]. Yes, dear. A going-away gift. And very sensible, too.

CORNELIA [*already disappointed*]. Oh.

MRS. SKINNER [*taking it out of the wrapping*]. See, dear? A safety-pocket!

CORNELIA. A what?

OTIS. For your old razor blades.

MRS. SKINNER. You put your valuables in it. I'll show you.

[MRS. SKINNER *takes the things out of* CORNELIA'S *purse and empties them into the pocket.*]

CORNELIA. But—isn't it sort of—*big*, Mother?

MRS. SKINNER. No bigger than your purse, dear——

CORNELIA. But—the long strap. What's that for?

MRS. SKINNER. Why, to fasten it around your waist, of course! [*She slips it around* CORNELIA'S *waist.*]

CORNELIA. But, Mother—it's—it's heavy—I'd just as soon wear a papoose!

OTIS. Fortunately, you're not being faced with that alternative.

MRS. SKINNER. Cornelia, don't talk nonsense! Nobody's going to see it.

CORNELIA. Nobody's going to see it! How are they going to *miss* it? They'll be lucky if they're not *struck* with it every time I turn a corner!

MRS. SKINNER. But, baby! You wear it *inside* the dress! Like this!

[MRS. SKINNER *backs* CORNELIA *into a position where we cannot see the operation as she stuffs it inside her skirt.*]

MRS. SKINNER. It's the only safe way. I've read it in the papers about these young girls being accosted by bandits and brigands!

OTIS. Although conditions *have* improved since the Spanish Main. [*He has been getting restless in the doorway.*] I'll bet Emily *is* on board someplace. [*He disappears down the corridor, calling.*] Emily! Emily Kimbrough! Come out, come out, wherever you are!

[OTIS'S *voice fades as* MRS. SKINNER *completes the operation and steps aside.*]

MRS. SKINNER. There, now! You see? Nobody will ever notice it!

CORNELIA [*taking steps to try it, and sinking fast*]. Notice it! Look at that bulge! They'll think I'm a smuggler!

MRS. SKINNER [*unshaken*]. Cornelia, it's a necessary precaution. I want you to promise me you'll wear it all the time.

CORNELIA [*tragically*]. Oh, no, no! Mother, please! *Don't* make me promise!

MRS. SKINNER. Otherwise, I won't have a moment's peace about you.

CORNELIA. But, Mother, I'll never be able to face Emily!

MRS. SKINNER. Good heavens, why not?

CORNELIA. With a bean-bag bouncing around in my clothes? She'll think my parents are just plain primitive!

[OTIS *appears in the doorway, up center, loaded with wrapped packages.*]

OTIS. I *knew* she was on board and couldn't find her way! She was just heading into the boiler room.

[*As* OTIS *steps out of the doorway, coming into the room, he reveals* EMILY *directly behind him. She has a basket of fruit in one hand and a dress on a hanger in the other.*]

EMILY. Hello, everybody!

CORNELIA [*sinking onto the bunk with a groan and hiding the bulge*]. Em-ily!

MRS. SKINNER. There you are, Emily! We thought you were lost!

EMILY [*breezing into the room unconcernedly, letting* MRS. SKINNER *give her a peck on the cheek and running right on*]. Hello, Mrs. Skinner! No, I wasn't lost. Just misdirected. But he was so handsome while he was giving me the directions, I guess I didn't listen very carefully, and then I took a wrong turn. Hello, Cornelia! Mr. Skinner, you can just put those things down there. [*She indicates the chaise longue.*] And thanks ever so much.

MRS. SKINNER [*as* OTIS *unloads*]. We don't really have another moment to stay now. How is your mother, Emily?

EMILY. Oh, just fine! She saw me to the train in Muncie. Oh! I almost forgot! [*She goes to the chaise longue and begins to scatter the packages* OTIS *has put down.*] She gave me a book to give you for *your* trip. Oh, dear! Where *have* I put it?

MRS. SKINNER. Well, you don't have to bother, dear——

EMILY. Now, isn't that just like me! I opened it to read on the train, and then I wrapped it up again so you wouldn't notice, and now I don't remember which it is!

OTIS. Think nothing of it, Emily. We have a couple of extra timetables we can read.

EMILY [*blandly accepting this*]. Oh, then, that's fine! I'll give it to you in Paris, and you can read it on the way back. [*She flops down on the chaise longue.*] Oh, it's so *good* to be off!

MRS. SKINNER. I'm sure, now, your mother has given you all the necessary instructions——

EMILY [*sitting up quickly*]. Oh, yes, Mrs. Skinner! All of them.

MRS. SKINNER [*turning to* CORNELIA, *who rises and comes to her*]. And you'll remember everything I've told *you*, baby?

CORNELIA. Yes, Mother, I will.

MRS. SKINNER [*kissing* CORNELIA]. Good-bye, dear.

CORNELIA [*as both girls become very grave, with the parting at hand*]. Good-bye, Mother.

MRS. SKINNER [*kissing* EMILY]. Good-bye, Emily.

EMILY. Good-bye, Mrs. Skinner. And Mr. Skinner.

OTIS [*kissing* CORNELIA]. Good-bye, girls. You know our hotel in Paris, don't you?

CORNELIA. Yes, Father.

EMILY. Yes, Mr. Skinner. I have it written down in three places.

[MRS. SKINNER *sniffs and goes out, up center.*]

OTIS. Be sure to call us the minute you arrive.

[CORNELIA *and* EMILY *nod gravely.*]

OTIS. If that won't be too much of a strain on your emancipation.

[OTIS *winks at* CORNELIA *and* EMILY *and goes out, up center. The girls are silent for a moment, staring at the door, just a little dazed now that the time is here; then they turn to each other—hold for second, and then scream, shrilly, and throw themselves into each other's arms.*]

CORNELIA. Emily!

EMILY. Cornelia! We're adrift!

CORNELIA [*as they dive onto the chaise longue into school-girlish positions*]. Alone on the wide, wide sea!

EMILY. And without our mothers here to cluck over us every minute!

CORNELIA. Isn't it wonderful? Did you ever really believe it'd finally happen?

EMILY. And when we go back to Bryn Mawr in September! . . .

CORNELIA. Won't the girls simply swoon with envy!

EMILY. And Cornelia! You're going to take lessons from Monsieur de la Croix in Paris! The one you saw in the magazine. Do you suppose he'd take me?

CORNELIA. Oh, Emily, *you're* not going to be an actress!

EMILY. Well, I thought it might help me with my dancing. Make it more expressive.

CORNELIA. And after this trip, we'll be different!

EMILY. Once you've been to Paris, you're *cosmopolitan!*

CORNELIA. I'm feeling cosmopolitan already.

[*There is a knock at the door, interrupting* CORNELIA *and* EMILY. *They break off sharply, taking relaxed, poised attitudes, very cosmopolitan.*]

EMILY [*calling out in worldly tones*]. Ye-es?

CORNELIA [*ditto*]. You may come!

[*The* STEWARD *enters, up center, with a valise.*]

STEWARD. Your valise, Miss Skinner.

CORNELIA [*forgetting, diving for it*]. Oh, good! I'll want that right away! [*She pulls up short as she realizes that she hasn't been very cosmopolitan, and relaxes graciously.*] You may put it down somewhere. Anywhere at all.

STEWARD [*setting it down near the bunks*]. Yes, miss. May I have your tags, Miss Kimbrough?

EMILY. Oh. [*She remembers her manner, too.*] Surely you may. I have them here, I think.

[EMILY *gets the tags out of her purse and hands them over to the* STEWARD *rather elegantly.*]

CORNELIA [*airily*]. I'm having all my trunks brought in, dear. I think it's best.

EMILY. Oh, very well. [*She continues with a gesture.*] All mine, too, Steward. Please.

[*The* STEWARD *looks a little green.*]

STEWARD. Yes, miss. [*He goes to* CORNELIA, *standing expectantly, as before.*] Will there be anything else, miss?

CORNELIA [*getting it this time*]. Oh! . . . Oh, yes, of course!

[CORNELIA *reaches for her purse, opens it, and then stops, realizing where her money is. She glances down at the bulge, which she has for the moment forgotten. She is embarrassed, but tries to cover up.*]

CORNELIA. Oh—uh—Emily, dear! Could I have a word with you?

[CORNELIA *makes a furtive gesture for* EMILY *to come over into the corner with her.*]

EMILY [*puzzled, but coming over*]. Certainly, dear. What is it?

CORNELIA [*in the corner, sotto voce, as the* STEWARD *looks away, professionally*]. Emily, would you tip him? I'll give it back to you later.

EMILY. Oh, sure!

[EMILY *starts for her purse, then suddenly stops in the middle of the room, and turns front, slowly. We see that she now has a peculiar expression on her face, too. She goes back to* CORNELIA, *and now also speaks sotto voce.*]

EMILY. Cornelia, are you *sure* you haven't got any loose change?

CORNELIA. Well, I have, but I can't get at it just this minute.

EMILY. Well, you see, that's exactly *my* trouble. I——

[*Suddenly,* EMILY *stops and looks at* CORNELIA, *who has just that moment looked at her; their mouths start to fall open simultaneously, and the light dawns. They instinctively cover their mouths with their hands and draw back, staring at each other.*]

CORNELIA [*in a hoarse whisper*]. Emily!

EMILY [*same*]. Cornelia!

CORNELIA. Did your mother————?

EMILY. Have you got one, too?

[*The* STEWARD *clears his throat.* CORNELIA *and* EMILY *jump at the sound. Then* CORNELIA *takes matters into her hands, striding toward him.*]

CORNELIA. My good man. Would you just—uh—go along, and bring on the trunks?

STEWARD [*surprised, and not pleased*]. Yes, miss. Certainly, miss.

[*The* STEWARD *leaves swiftly, up center, closing the door.* EMILY *and* CORNELIA *turn to each other.*]

CORNELIA. It's not possible!

EMILY. It *is* possible! [*She kicks her knee back and forth to show the bulge.*] Look!

CORNELIA. And look!

[CORNELIA *does the same. The two girls shriek in common horror and put their hands to their faces.*]

CORNELIA. I feel like the Ancient Mariner with the albatross strapped to my waist!

EMILY. Or the Spartan boy with the fox under his tunic!

CORNELIA. Isn't it *savage?*

EMILY. Weren't they just *fiends?*

CORNELIA. Emily, this calls for action.

EMILY [*nodding stoutly*]. I won't tell if you don't!

[EMILY *and* CORNELIA *march with great determination into the bathroom, and we hear their conversation from there as they remove their pockets.*]

CORNELIA. I didn't exactly *promise* I'd wear it. My father interrupted in the nick of time.

EMILY. My mother never does get me to promise anything. She can't keep up with me in a conversation.

CORNELIA. I'm going to get rid of mine—forever!

[EMILY *emerges from the bathroom, followed by* CORNELIA, *both carrying their safety-pockets.*]

EMILY. That's a good idea.

CORNELIA. Where'll we throw them?

EMILY [*going to the porthole*]. I wonder if this porthole is locked.

CORNELIA. Don't do that! You might let the sea in. [*She opens the door to the corridor, experimentally.*] Emily!

EMILY [*running to the door*]. What?

[CORNELIA *opens the door full. Outside, in the corridor, is a service tray on wheels, stacked with dishes and dish-covers. The girls exchange glances.*]

EMILY. Do we dare?

CORNELIA [*taking* EMILY'S *safety-pocket*]. Be of stout heart.

[CORNELIA *steps into the corridor, looking to make sure no one is watching, and then slips the pockets under a metal dish-cover. She scurries back in and shuts the door.*]

CORNELIA. There! I feel positively unshackled! [*She opens her valise.*] You know, Emily, I haven't decided yet what I'm going to be on this trip.

EMILY. What do you mean—what you're going to be?

CORNELIA. Well, the whole point about a trip on a boat is that there isn't time for people to get to know you. So you have to assume a very definite personality, or you won't emerge at all!

EMILY [*while putting away some of her packages*]. I see.

CORNELIA. I just got a present of the most wonderful long, dangling earrings. [*She holds up a dress out of the valise.*] And my new black dress is really almost slinky.

EMILY. It *is?*

CORNELIA. Well, yes, if I pull the belt very tight. Anyhow, I've been thinking. It might be interesting to be the *femme fatale* type. Like Theda Bara.

EMILY. Theda Bara?

CORNELIA. Can't you picture it? A woman in black. A tinge of sadness in her smile. Mysteriously alone in the moonlight. And a whiff of exotic perfume as she passes.

EMILY. Do you have the perfume, too?

CORNELIA. Yes. I bought a fourth of an ounce. [*She heads for the bathroom.*] I'm going to try it.

[*There is a knock at the door, up center.*]

CORNELIA. Emily, you answer it.

[CORNELIA *goes into the bathroom and shuts the door.*]

EMILY. Sure.

[EMILY *swings the door open blithely to face the* PURSER *of the ship and a ship's* STEWARDESS. *Both are looking very serious.*]

EMILY. Oh, hello!

PURSER. Miss Skinner?

EMILY. No, I'm Miss Kimbrough. Cornelia's in the—in there. [*She points to the bathroom.*]

PURSER. May I see your passports?

EMILY. Oh, why, certainly. They're right here someplace.

[EMILY *goes to their purses on the table as the* STEWARDESS *goes to the bathroom, pulling the door slightly ajar and calling in.*]

STEWARDESS. Anyone in there with you, Miss Skinner?

CORNELIA [*loudly, from inside*]. Of course not! Who wants to know?

EMILY [*yelling across the room*]. They want to see our passports, Cornelia. In case we're stowaways, or something!

PURSER [*sharply*]. Who told you that? How did you know?

EMILY [*agape*]. How did I know what?

[*The* STEWARDESS *is now busily inspecting the entire cabin, checking bunks, etc.* EMILY *drops the purses on the chaise longue.*]

PURSER. That there's a stowaway aboard.

EMILY. Oh, but I didn't know!

PURSER [*checking himself, realizing his blunder*]. Oh, well, there is. We're checking all the cabins now.

STEWARDESS. Keep an eye out. Report anything suspicious.

EMILY [*thrilled*]. Are you the police?

PURSER. No. Ship's purser, miss.

[*The* STEWARDESS *goes out, up center.*]

PURSER. Now, if possible, we don't want this to get around. Disturb the passengers. As far as you're concerned, this is a routine passport checkup.

EMILY [*wide-eyed*]. I understand. I won't say a word!

[*The* PURSER *nods and, with a last glance around the cabin, goes out, up center.* EMILY *flies to the bathroom door, shouting through it.*]

EMILY. Cornelia! Cornelia! There's a stowaway on board!

CORNELIA [*popping the door open and just sticking her head out*]. What?

EMILY. Yes? Think of it!

CORNELIA. Emily! Adventure already!

[CORNELIA *pops her head back in.* EMILY *starts for the chaise longue to return the passports to the purses.*]

EMILY. *Won't* we have stories to tell? [*She is putting the passports back when she halts, looking up, suddenly.*] Cornelia! I'm going out and watch.

CORNELIA [*shouting from inside*]. Watch?

EMILY. They're hot on the trail of that stowaway. I want to be in on the kill.

[EMILY *runs to the door, up center, and opens it just as the* STEWARD *is about to knock. It looks as though he were going to strike her. She leaps back, squealing, and then pulls herself together.*]

STEWARD. I'm starting with the trunks, miss.

EMILY. Oh. [*She speaks very confidentially.*] I won't say a word about the stowaway.

[EMILY *goes out, up center. The* STEWARD *removes his cap and scratches his head, puzzled.*]

CORNELIA [*shouting from the bathroom*]. Who's there?

STEWARD. Steward, miss. Where do you want this trunk?

CORNELIA. Oh! [*She pauses slightly. When she speaks there is a marked change of voice, toward the sultry and worldly.*] Just a moment. I'll be out.

STEWARD. Yes, miss.

[*The* STEWARD *starts to angle the trunk into the room, turned away from the bathroom.* CORNELIA *appears in the doorway. She is in her slinky black dress, pulled tight at the belt, has long earrings on, and a pale make-up. She leans sadly against the door frame and speaks in a somewhat broken voice.*]

CORNELIA. Just put it—anywhere, Steward. Anywhere at all.

[*The* STEWARD *turns at the voice, and does a take, his eyes popping.*]

STEWARD. Oh, I beg your pardon. I thought it was Miss Skinner. I——[*He then takes a closer look.*] Why, it *is* Miss Skinner!

CORNELIA [*sadly, crossing the stage and sitting in a depressed fashionable manner*]. Yes. Yes. One can't escape *that*, can one?

[*The* STEWARD *just stares at* CORNELIA. *Then he settles the trunk at right stage, watching her peculiarly over his shoulder, and starts for the door. As he is about to exit,* CORNELIA *lets a sudden, soulful sigh escape her. The* STEWARD *hesitates, wondering.*]

STEWARD. Is—is anything the matter, miss?

CORNELIA [*giving it the Theda Bara touch*]. Oh, no. No, no.
You needn't be concerned about me.

[*The* STEWARD *nods, fishily, and attempts to go again, but once
more* CORNELIA *speaks.*]

CORNELIA. I'm really quite over it now.

STEWARD. *Was* something wrong, miss? It's my business to see
that everyone is comfortable.

CORNELIA. Comfortable? [*She laughs bitterly and walks away
from the* STEWARD.] What can you know of comfort? [*She
turns toward the* STEWARD *suddenly.*] Don't worry. I'm not
going to bore you with my story. [*She turns away again,
playing with a long handkerchief.*] After all, what is there
to say, now? Why stir up old embers? Poor Geoffrey.

STEWARD [*vainly trying to grasp this*]. Geoffrey?

CORNELIA [*working around the room and touching things, as
though highstrung*]. Yes, I could never tell my parents, of
course. They'd never have understood Geoffrey. He always
played for high stakes, you see. And then—one June evening
when the moon was very bright——

[*The* STEWARD *starts to back toward the door.*]

CORNELIA. —he put everything on number seven. And lost.

STEWARD [*feeling for the door, nodding strangely*]. I see.

CORNELIA. It was all rather tragic. And, of course, he couldn't
marry me, then.

STEWARD [*getting a good grip on the doorknob and starting to
back through*]. No. Of course not.

CORNELIA. Not that I wouldn't have been content in the
château. What if there were no servants—only old Pedro?
I would have been happy to live on wild berries, and goat's
milk. But he had his pride.

STEWARD. Yes, miss.

[*As the* STEWARD *backs out the door, up center, he backs smack
into* EMILY, *who is returning. He jumps.*]

STEWARD. Uh!

EMILY [*unconcernedly*]. We didn't catch the stowaway. He eluded us.

STEWARD [*turning into the room*]. I think you'd better see to Miss Skinner, miss. She seems unhappy about something.

[*The* STEWARD *goes out, up center.* EMILY *does not understand what he means.*]

EMILY. Huh? [*She notices the dress and earrings.*] Cornelia! Oh-h-h, Cornelia! It's devastating! You look just like a widow who's traveling with her husband's ashes!

CORNELIA [*reflective now*]. Well, Emily, I don't know. I think he was *impressed,* all right, but do I really want to be remote and on a pedestal?

[*While listening,* EMILY *goes to the bunks, inspecting them.*]

CORNELIA. I'm afraid everybody just might leave me alone in my grief.

EMILY [*discovering a life preserver under the bunks and forgetting all about* CORNELIA'S *problem*]. Oh! I always wanted to see a life preserver! Here are the instructions!

[EMILY *starts to read the instructions, delighted, as* CORNELIA *begins to take off her earrings.*]

CORNELIA. Besides, these earrings sort of pinch.

EMILY. It says that this life preserver is to be used only in case of emergency. What kind of an emergency, Cornelia?

CORNELIA. In case the boat sinks, silly.

EMILY. Hm. That's what I thought. You know, until this minute it never occurred to me that boats sank any more.

CORNELIA. For heaven's sake, why not?

EMILY [*standing up and putting the life preserver around her and getting it on wrong*]. I don't know. I only think of historical boats sinking. Like the *Nina* or the *Pinta,* or the *Hesperus.*

CORNELIA [*starting for the bathroom*]. Emily, I can just see the burning deck, whence all but you had fled.

[*There is a knock on the door, up center, and the* STEWARD'S *voice is heard immediately.*]

STEWARD. Another trunk, miss!

[CORNELIA *scoots into the bathroom.*]

EMILY [*strapping the preserver on herself*]. Bring it in.

[*The door opens and the* STEWARD *backs in, lugging a heavy trunk.*]

EMILY. Steward, am I getting this on right?

[*The* STEWARD *turns and sees what* EMILY *is up to. His eyes go heavenwards.*]

STEWARD. Oh, my word! [*He swings the trunk into any old position and starts to get out of the room.*] Yes—yes—I think so, miss. . . .

[*The* STEWARD *goes out swiftly, up center, leaving the door open.*]

EMILY [*going toward the door, still fixing the preserver*]. Well, now *he* acted awfully peculiar! What do you suppose has got into him?

[*As* EMILY *stands in the doorway, facing into the cabin,* DICK WINTERS, *another passenger, passes by on the way to his cabin, his suitcase in hand. He sees* EMILY *all strapped up, does a double-take, and comes back to look closer.*]

DICK. Ye gods! We're not sinking already?

EMILY [*very embarrassed*]. Oh, no! I don't think so. I—I was just trying it on. [*She has started to back into the room, but now sees that he is quite a good-looking young man, and her expression changes, as she thinks of something to continue the conversation.*] I—uh—would you know if I've got it on right?

DICK [*with casual amusement*]. Well, I don't know. It depends on whether you're going to play halfback or tackle.

EMILY [*informatively*]. Oh, *this* is a life preserver.

DICK [*with a light, friendly sarcasm that is lost on* EMILY]. Oh, of course. How stupid of me. I can see that now.

EMILY. I know it's all very silly of me. There's not really much chance that the boat will sink.

DICK. Hm? No. I don't think so. [*He decides to have some fun.*] I hear there hasn't been a sinking in several weeks.

EMILY [*gulping*]. Oh? *Was* there a sinking several weeks ago? I don't remember hearing about it.

DICK. Well, they keep it out of the papers, you see. Afraid it'll scare people about taking trips.

EMILY [*far from happy*]. Oh. . . .

DICK. Of course, people are foolish to be scared. Just because one out of every four boats hits an iceberg, it doesn't mean that *we* will.

EMILY [*green*]. Oh, no, we'd never hit an iceberg!

DICK. Besides, why worry about it? If we did, what chance would *we* have to get out—way down here?

EMILY [*trying to laugh it off*]. Not—much at all, I don't suppose.

DICK. But I'll tell you what. If you should hear a *crunching* sound anytime after we get started, let us know. My friend and I—we're right around the corner. Ta-ta.

[DICK *grins and goes out, up center.* EMILY *shuts the door in great terror and runs to the bathroom door.*]

EMILY. Cornelia! Cornelia! There are icebergs!

[CORNELIA *rushes out, her make-up more youthful and her hair more normal.*]

CORNELIA. Where? *Where?*

EMILY. Not yet. Not yet. But there will be.

CORNELIA. Who told you?

EMILY [*suddenly switching her concentration completely*]. Oh, Cornelia! The best-looking boy. Right around the corner. I'll see if I can arrange an introduction for *you*. [*She is suddenly perturbed.*] Cornelia! Did your mother say anything to you about strange men?

CORNELIA. No. Except that I wasn't to talk to them.

EMILY. That's just it! So did mine. Now, here's the thing, Cornelia. Technically, any man we don't know is a strange man. Does that mean we can't talk to a man all summer?

CORNELIA. Heavens, no! Our mothers just mean gigolos and jewel thieves—types like that.

[*There is a knock on the door.*]

EMILY [*happily*]. Oh, we're meeting more people!

[EMILY *throws open the door and there stands a very impressive looking man in a fancy uniform, his hands behind his back. Because he looks as though he ought to be at least an Admiral, we will call him that for the moment. He has a beautiful continental accent.*]

ADMIRAL [*bowing*]. I understand that this cabin is occupied by Miss Skinner and Miss Kimbrough. Is that correct?

CORNELIA [*impressed, in her best manner*]. That is correct, sir.

ADMIRAL [*bowing*]. Excellent! Then I shall be able to perform a service for two very charming ladies.

[EMILY *and* CORNELIA *are much taken in. They laugh charmingly.*]

EMILY. Oh. Shall you? [*She hurriedly gets out of her life preserver.*]

ADMIRAL. Yes, indeed! I hope that you have not been too seriously inconvenienced by your loss.

CORNELIA. Our loss?

ADMIRAL. I am very happy to be able to return these to you.

[*The* ADMIRAL *produces the two safety-pockets.* CORNELIA *and* EMILY *blanch.*]

ADMIRAL. They *are* yours, aren't they?

CORNELIA [*very embarrassed, taking them and hiding them quickly*]. Why—uh—why, yes! I suppose so.

EMILY [*also embarrassed*]. Oh, dear! Where did you find them?

ADMIRAL [*charmingly*]. You'll never believe this, ladies, but they were reported to have turned up in the kitchen. Our wide-awake personnel saw immediately that they were articles of consequence. And the name Kimbrough was stamped inside one of them, so—you—see—it was really a very simple matter.

EMILY. Well, I—I'm sure you meant it very kindly.

ADMIRAL. I am *delighted* to have been of service. Now, before I go—perhaps you will think this too personal——

CORNELIA [*eagerly, playing up to him*]. Oh, *no!*

ADMIRAL. Well, I confess to having a certain curiosity about the little bags. May I ask—what exactly are they?

CORNELIA [*embarrassed again, covering up fast*]. Why, how funny that you should ask that! So many people do! Don't they, Emily?

[EMILY *tries to agree, laughingly, but without much success.*]

CORNELIA. It's rather an involved explanation.

ADMIRAL. Oh, really?

CORNELIA. Yes. You see—my great, great uncle. That's my uncle on my mother's side of the family. He was an Indian fighter.

ADMIRAL. You don't say!

CORNELIA. Of course, he didn't always fight Indians.

EMILY [*trying to help*]. Sometimes there would be whole years when they would just sit around smoking peace pipes.

CORNELIA. Anyhow, when he wasn't fighting Indians, he sometimes carried mail to the colonies. Not all the mail, understand—just cards, and things. And he carried them in those bags. So they're rather family heirlooms, you see.

ADMIRAL. My! What a curious history! Well! I mustn't keep you, must I? I'll no doubt see you on deck, ladies. Good day!

[*The* ADMIRAL *goes out, up center, with* CORNELIA *to the door, calling after him.*]

CORNELIA. Good day! And thanks. Thanks awfully! [*She comes back in, closes the door, and squeals with delight.*] And wasn't *he* handsome? Emily, he was at least an Admiral!

EMILY. Do you really think so? [*She frowns.*] Cornelia. Maybe we should have given him a tip.

CORNELIA. Heavens! You don't tip Admirals!

EMILY. Yes, but we don't *know* he's an Admiral. I'd better offer it to him, anyway.

[EMILY *runs to the door.*]

CORNELIA. Emily! Let *me!*

[EMILY *runs out, up center, as* CORNELIA *starts to run after her. There is a crash in the corridor.* CORNELIA *hurries to the doorway, horrified as she looks out.*]

CORNELIA. Emily! What are you doing on the floor?

[*There is a groan from* EMILY, *and as* CORNELIA *backs into the cabin,* EMILY *appears, limping, rubbing her hipbone, and holding a pair of men's shoes in her hand. She closes the door behind her.*]

EMILY. Look at that! Now, who'd leave a pair of shoes right out in the corridor?

CORNELIA. Oh, you gave me such a fright!

[*There is a knock on the door, and then the* STEWARD'S *voice is heard.*]

STEWARD. Trunk, miss!

CORNELIA [*suddenly realizing*]. Emily! Don't let him see you with a pair of men's shoes! Hide them!

[EMILY *starts in several directions, frantically looking for a hiding place, and then desperately throws them to* CORNELIA. CORNELIA, *dismayed, throws them on the lower bunk and both girls dive to a sitting position there, covering the shoes. They swing their legs with great nonchalance as the* STEWARD *backs in with another trunk. When he happens to glance at them, they grin broadly and foolishly, with false innocence. The spectacle is too much for him and he hurries out.* CORNELIA *jumps up.*]

CORNELIA. Emily! What'll we do with them?

[*Suddenly, a very loud horn is heard, above.* EMILY *jumps.*]

EMILY. What's that? Are we sinking?

[*There is band music above.*]

CORNELIA. No! Emily! We're sailing!

EMILY. What? [*She forgets all about the shoes.*] Oh, Cornelia, this is terrible! I intended to be on deck when we sailed, so I could be emotional!

CORNELIA. Emotional?

EMILY. If I was up there, I *know* I'd get a lump in my throat as I saw my native land slipping over the horizon!

CORNELIA. Of course, our native land stays still. We slip over the horizon!

EMILY. But I wanted to see it becoming a speck in the distance! [*She speaks with quick determination.*] I'm going up! [*She bolts for the door.*]

CORNELIA. I've got to change my dress first.

EMILY. Oh, I know! [*She suddenly reverses her course, runs back, and snatches up her safety-pocket.*] And I know how I'm going to get rid of mine! Overboard!

[EMILY *is now out the door, up center, and gone.*]

CORNELIA. Well! You might have taken mine! [*She starts for the bathroom.*]

[HARRIET *and* WINIFRED, *two English girls from a neighboring cabin, appear in the open doorway, briskly, and barge right along in.* CORNELIA *stops, and turns, staring.*]

HARRIET. I say there! I hate most awfully to bother you!

[HARRIET *immediately goes to the water cabinet and begins to wash her hands.* WINIFRED *follows her, as they talk.*]

CORNELIA. Uh—hello——

WINIFRED. It really is a bit of an imposition, don't you know.

CORNELIA. What is?

[CORNELIA *remembers the shoes and tries to hide them, but is almost caught in the attempt.*]

HARRIET [*brushing her teeth*]. Let us explain. I'm Harriet St. John, and this is Winifred Blaugh.

WINIFRED. We're neighbors of yours.

HARRIET. Matter of fact, just two cabins down.

WINIFRED [*gargling*]. Next to those very smart-looking American boys.

CORNELIA. I—see.

WINIFRED [*wiping her hands on one of* CORNELIA'S *towels*]. And we're jolly well in a difficulty.

HARRIET. Our water basin. The beastly thing won't work.

WINIFRED [*having just about completed her toilet*]. Might we use yours?

CORNELIA. Oh—oh, certainly! Help yourself.

HARRIET. Extremely decent of you.

WINIFRED. I have to brush my teeth. Do you have the dentifrice, Harriet?

HARRIET. Righto. It's most frightfully inconvenient. We can't even pour out a tumbler of water for ourselves!

CORNELIA. That's too bad.

The curtain on the first act of "Our Hearts Were Young and Gay," as produced at The Catholic University Theatre, Washington, D.C.

WINIFRED [*finishing brushing her teeth*]. Well, it's been frightfully ripping of you!

HARRIET [*as they start to the door again*]. Yes, frightfully!

CORNELIA [*going to the door, to hurry them out*]. Oh, you're
quite welcome. Do come again.

[CORNELIA *has practically got* HARRIET *and* WINIFRED *out when
there are sudden, very loud shouts from above.* CORNELIA
*swings the door open again, and the three girls stand and
listen, terrified.*]

CORNELIA. What's that?

HARRIET .What's he saying?

WINIFRED. Harriet! He's saying "Man overboard!"

[*The shouts become clearer. They do say "Man overboard!"*]

HARRIET. Someone's gone over the side.

CORNELIA. Oh, good lord! Emily!

WINIFRED. Emily? Who's Emily?

CORNELIA. My roommate! She just went up on deck! And she
doesn't swim very well!

HARRIET. Of course, they're shouting "*Man* overboard," you
know.

WINIFRED. Yes, but Harriet, dear, they always say that. It could
mean *either* sex.

CORNELIA [*as they are blocking the door*]. Oh, let me by,
please! I've got to see!

[*As* WINIFRED *and* HARRIET *break, the* ADMIRAL *appears in the
corridor, further blocking* CORNELIA.]

ADMIRAL. Miss Skinner. Ladies. I must request all passengers
to remain in their cabins during the emergency.

CORNELIA [*overwrought*]. Oh, could you tell me—please—
who went overboard?

ADMIRAL. I'm sorry. We're not allowed to divulge that infor-
mation until they've recovered the body.

CORNELIA [*with a wail*]. Oh! The body!

ADMIRAL. The horn will be sounded at such time as passengers are permitted to return to the deck. Stand by.

[*The* ADMIRAL *quickly departs on his rounds.*]

HARRIET. Don't carry on, dear. It's surely not Emily.

[CORNELIA *is tearing a handkerchief to shreds and biting it, tearfully.*]

WINIFRED. I do hope not. They usually drown when they go over, you know.

[*There is another wail from* CORNELIA.]

WINIFRED. What a beastly shame that *would* be!

HARRIET [*punching* CORNELIA's *shoulder*]. Buck up, girl! We'd best slip back to our own cabin, now.

WINIFRED. Lucky thing we were here to console her, what?

HARRIET [*calling back to* CORNELIA, *at the door*]. Give us a call if you need us, dear. Stout fella, now!

[HARRIET *and* WINIFRED *go out, up center, closing the door.* CORNELIA *is tortured, and she paces, moaning.*]

CORNELIA. Emily! Emily! You should have been taking swimming, instead of dancing! I told you! [*She suddenly runs to a porthole, trying to see through it.*] No, no, no. Can't see a thing. And all that seaweed!

[*There is a sudden sound of light, rapid footsteps racing down the stairs.* CORNELIA *starts, and turns toward the door, breathless. A few more footsteps are heard in the corridor, and then* EMILY *slips in, up center, closing the door tightly behind her, wide-eyed.*]

CORNELIA. Emily!

EMILY [*desperately, leaning on the door, breathing hard*]. Sh-h-h! Quiet!

CORNELIA [*going to* EMILY]. Emily, you gave me such a fright! When I heard all that shouting and screaming, I was sure it was you!

EMILY [*feverishly*]. How did you know?

CORNELIA. How did I know what?

EMILY [*panting, terrified*]. That it was me.

CORNELIA. Then it *was* you?

EMILY. Yes, Cornelia, I did it.

CORNELIA. But you couldn't have fallen overboard! You're not even wet!

EMILY. Oh, Cornelia, it's much worse than that. Cornelia——

CORNELIA [*breathless now, too*]. Yes?

EMILY. I killed a man.

CORNELIA [*gasping, and stepping back*]. Who? What man?

EMILY. The man that fell overboard.

CORNELIA. Emily! You didn't *push* him?

EMILY [*between breaths, reliving the whole horrible sequence*]. I was on deck. All of a sudden there was a splash and a lot of commotion. Somebody shouted "Man overboard!" So I ran to the rail like everybody else. And there he was! I could see him—down in that dark water, splashing and swimming. Oh, he looked so pathetic—clawing the water and kicking his stockinged feet. Then, I remembered what they told us in lifesaving class. Throw a buoyant object to the person who is drowning. But I couldn't find a buoyant object. All I could find was a deck chair.

CORNELIA [*realizing the full horror*]. Emily! You didn't throw the deck chair?

EMILY. I did. And, Cornelia. It hit him. Right on the head.

CORNELIA. I don't believe it! Your aim was never that good! How do you know it hit him?

EMILY. Just at that moment—they turned on the searchlights! And everybody could see it crash!

CORNELIA [*turning away, her hands to her head*]. Oh, good heavens!

EMILY. It was horrible. You should have heard the crack when it landed on his head. And then there was just the chair, wobbling all around by itself—and no man. [*She begins to cry.*]

CORNELIA [*a sudden hope*]. Emily! Did anybody see you throw the chair?

EMILY. No. I was in the dark.

CORNELIA. Then, don't worry. We'll keep you under cover. No one need ever know.

EMILY [*biting her lip*]. No, Cornelia. I know what it is I must do. Give myself up!

CORNELIA. Oh, no, Emily!

EMILY. Yes. It would haunt me all my days.

CORNELIA. But, Emily, you don't *know* what they'll do to you!

EMILY. It doesn't make any difference. I have to confess. I couldn't live with my conscience. Cornelia, you must go and tell the Captain.

CORNELIA. Oh, Emily, I couldn't! I'd be an informer.

EMILY [*nobly*]. Please, Cornelia. Don't refuse me this. My knees are shaking so much I could never walk up the steps.

CORNELIA. Emily! [*She breaks.*] All right. If you really want me to.

EMILY. I'll be grateful as long as I live. Mercy! How long do you think they'll *let* me live!

CORNELIA. Don't say things like that!

EMILY. Cornelia, maybe there'll be an inquest. My goodness! Will they have it here on the ship or wait until we get to France? Cornelia, that would be terrible! I couldn't possibly testify in French.

[EMILY *is about to sink onto the bunk. She screams and jumps up.*]

CORNELIA. Emily! What now?

EMILY [*pointing, horrified, at the shoes*]. The shoes! The shoes!

CORNELIA. Oh, we've got worse things to think about than that!

EMILY. They're his! They must be! The man I killed! A dead man's shoes!

CORNELIA. But—how could they be?

EMILY. I don't know, but he didn't have any shoes on!

CORNELIA. I'll hide them.

EMILY. But why? When I'm going to confess! Oh, Cornelia, go—go, now! While I can still stand.

CORNELIA [*running to the door, finally, obediently*]. I'll bring him right down.

EMILY [*sinking onto the chaise longue*]. Thank you. Thank you, Cornelia.

[CORNELIA *runs out, up center, and closes the door.* EMILY *moans, staring front for a moment; then her chin steadies. She rises, and we realize she is preparing her speech for the Captain.*]

EMILY. Captain . . . Captain. I'm ready to go. [*She puts her hands forward, as though to be manacled.*] I won't make any trouble. If you could only keep it out of the papers, so my mother won't know. Let me just disappear, quietly.

[*There is a rap on the door, up center.* EMILY *calls out, certain it is the Captain.*]

EMILY. All right. Come in. I'm not armed.

[DICK *opens the door and sticks his head in.*]

DICK. Hello, again!

EMILY [*wheeling around, startled*]. Oh! Oh, hello.

DICK. Say—you didn't happen to see anything of a pair of shoes, did you? My——

EMILY [*a big sob*]. Oh! The shoes! Yes!

DICK [*coming in*]. You did? Swell! You see, they belong to my friend and——

EMILY. O-o-h! Was he a friend of yours?

DICK. My roommate.

EMILY [*bursting into tears*]. And now he's dead! And you'll never forgive me!

DICK [*astounded, but still capable of taking it in his wisecracking stride*]. Dead? Oh, no, that's just his *expression*. He's not really dead.

EMILY. Oh, I see! They haven't told you about it yet! [*She goes to him, pitifully.*] Oh, I'm *so* sorry! Was he as young as you?

DICK [*puzzled, but patient*]. Oh, younger. But he's old enough to wear shoes.

EMILY [*turning away again, sobbing*]. I'd give them to you, too! I would! Only the Captain will need them as evidence!

DICK. Evidence? Now, look, dear, suppose we just sit down together and talk this whole thing out. [*He sits with her.*] I imagine your life has been difficult right from the beginning, hasn't it?

EMILY. Oh, you don't get the point at all.

DICK. How clever of you to put it that way. You certainly do have a knack for hitting things right on the head.

EMILY [*a bawl*]. Y-es. That's just it!

DICK. Ah, yes. Well, we'll count to ten and start back at the beginning. All right? Now, I came to get my friend's shoes.

EMILY. I know——

DICK. See? We *are* getting somewhere. Maybe I should explain that the only reason he wants these particular shoes is that he has a kind of sentimental attachment for them. They're the only pair he's got.

EMILY. Oh, dear! Then he'll want to be buried in them, won't he?

DICK [*giving up in despair*]. Uh-huh! That does it. I did my best. Well, from here in, friend Leo can collect his own shoes. [*He starts out.*]

EMILY. Good-bye.

DICK. Good-bye. And don't think it hasn't been charming.

[DICK *goes to the door, still staring back at* EMILY. *At the door,* DICK *barges into the* STEWARD, *bringing in another trunk.*]

DICK. Pardon me!

[DICK *goes out, up center.*]

STEWARD. Another trunk, miss.

EMILY [*looking up*]. Of course, I won't need it now.

STEWARD [*pop-eyed by this time*]. You *won't?*

EMILY. No, but leave it. That's all right. I want to have my treasures about me.

[*The* STEWARD *slaps his hand to his forehead, desperately, and goes out, up center, crossing* WINIFRED *on the way in, who sails to the washbasin cabinet, merely calling across to* EMILY, *not looking.*]

WINIFRED. Cheerio! Forgot the cap on my tube. Sorry to disturb.

[WINIFRED *starts back toward the door as* HARRIET *enters, up center.*]

HARRIET. Winifred, have you an aspirin? I've *such* a headache!

WINIFRED. It's a beastly crossing, isn't it——[*She glances at* EMILY *and realizes it isn't Cornelia.*] Oh, you're the other one!

[EMILY *is simply looking at them, dazed.*]

HARRIET [*looking, also*]. The one who went overboard?

EMILY. Oh, I didn't fall overboard! Who are you?

HARRIET [*to* WINIFRED]. You see, dear? I *told* that girl she hadn't gone overboard!

EMILY. But I'm the one who did it, though.

WINIFRED. Did it?

EMILY. Yes. I killed him.

WINIFRED *and* HARRIET [*simultaneously, moving toward* EMILY]. What?

[*There is a clatter of footsteps outside and of people coming down the corridor.* ALL *turn toward the door, up center.* CORNELIA *appears, leading the* PURSER *and the* STEW-ARDESS.]

CORNELIA. I couldn't find the Captain, Emily. Will he do?

PURSER [*striding into the cabin*]. Well, Miss Kimbrough! We meet again.

EMILY [*rising, wiping away a tear*]. Yes, your Majesty. Under *most* distressing circumstances!

PURSER [*going to* EMILY, *his moustache bristling and his hands snapping nervously in the manner of brisk authority*]. So you're the young lady who threw the deck chair overboard?

EMILY. Yes, sir. I admit it. I admit everything.

CORNELIA [*to the* STEWARDESS]. You will be tender with her, won't you?

PURSER. What *ever* made you think of doing a thing like that?

EMILY. A course I took. In lifesaving.

[*The* STEWARD *is backing into the room, unawares, with another trunk.*]

STEWARD [*forcing his way between the* STEWARDESS *and* COR-NELIA]. Pardon me, please. Another trunk.

[*The room is pretty full of trunks by this time, and everyone has to wind around and through them to get to anyone else.*]

PURSER [*distracted by this, and roaring*]. Steward! What the devil do you mean—bringing all these trunks in here?

STEWARD [*taking off his hat, in anguish, almost weeping*]. But they asked for them, sir! They *asked* for them!

EMILY [*bursting out into a wail*]. And to think I never even got to open mine!

PURSER [*turning back to* EMILY, *startled*]. Now, see here, young lady——

[LEO MCEVOY, *Dick's roommate, equally young and equally good-looking, but in his stocking feet, strides into the room from the corridor, and doesn't even wait to see what is going on.*]

LEO. Now, just a moment, everybody! *Who's got my shoes?*
PURSER [*exploding*]. Shoes? *Shoes?*
LEO. Now, come across! *Somebody* in here's got them, and I mean to know who!
EMILY. But they can't be yours! They're the dead man's!
LEO. The dead man's?
EMILY [*running to the bunk and producing the shoes, handing them toward the* PURSER]. Here they are, sir! I surrender them!
LEO. Surrender them? [*He snatches them out from under the* PURSER'S *nose.*] You'll surrender them to me, if you please!

[DICK *has strolled in, up center, and watches this with both concern and amusement.*]

PURSER. Now, just a minute there! What is all this about shoes?
LEO. Sir. All I did was put them out in the corridor for the Steward to pick up and shine——
EMILY. Is *that* how they got there? I thought——
PURSER. Miss Kimbrough, are you responsible for this, too?
EMILY. Yes, sir. I guess I'm responsible for *everything!*

[*The* ADMIRAL *has appeared in the doorway.*]

ADMIRAL. May I have a word with you?
CORNELIA [*calling across to the* PURSER, *who has been merely staring at* EMILY]. The Admiral wishes to speak with you.
PURSER [*turning around, wide-eyed, puffing*]. Admiral? What Admiral?
CORNELIA [*pointing to the* ADMIRAL, *who is himself dumbfounded by the designation*]. Him!
PURSER. *Admiral!* He's the leader of the ship's band!

[CORNELIA *collapses on the chaise longue with a loud groan.*]

PURSER. Just a moment, Hodges. I haven't finished with this young lady yet. [*He turns back to* EMILY, *who quakes.*]

EMILY. I'm ready, sir. [*She shuts her eyes tight.*]

PURSER. Well! What I came down here to tell you—before all these interruptions got started—is that we all owe you a debt of gratitude.

EMILY [*her eyes popping open, leaning toward the* PURSER, *to hear better*]. Huh?

PURSER. The man upon whom you scored such a magnificent bull's-eye was the stowaway we've been looking for!

EMILY. Oh!

PURSER. Why, if you hadn't hit him and knocked him unconscious, we might never have gotten him into a lifeboat!

EMILY. Unconscious? Then he's not dead?

PURSER. Certainly not. He is now in the brig, under guard. Stowing away is a criminal offense, you know. There may even be some kind of reward for you in this!

[EMILY *is now reeling slightly.*]

EMILY. Cornelia!

[CORNELIA *runs to* EMILY, *steadying her.*]

PURSER. In any case, Miss Kimbrough, you may be sure that we appreciate your foresightedness very much. [*He snaps to a salute.*]

EMILY [*dazed*]. You hear that, Cornelia? They appreciate my foresightedness very much.

CORNELIA [*having difficulty holding her up*]. Yes, Emily, I hear——

EMILY [*collapsing and bawling aloud*]. Oh, Cornelia! I was so scared!

CORNELIA [*right down beside* EMILY, *crying, too*]. I know, Emily! So was I!

PURSER. *What* in heaven's name has gotten into the girls? Eh?

[DICK *and* LEO *run to* EMILY *and* CORNELIA. *One of them pinches* EMILY'S *wrist to stir the circulation. The* PURSER *turns to the* ADMIRAL, *baffled.*]

PURSER. Hodges! Did you have something for me?

ADMIRAL. Yes, sir.

[*The* ADMIRAL *and the* PURSER *go into a private whispered conversation.*]

EMILY. What would they have thought in Muncie, Indiana?

DICK [*soothing* EMILY]. Now, now, now—you're going to be all right.

LEO. With a good night's sleep and a nice, vigorous game of deck tennis tomorrow, you'll forget the whole thing happened!

EMILY [*coming to, wiping her eyes*]. Deck tennis?

DICK. Sure! How about a game?

LEO [*to* CORNELIA]. We'll make it a foursome.

EMILY. Oh, *she* couldn't play deck tennis. She's too sultry!

[CORNELIA *pokes* EMILY *to be quiet.*]

PURSER [*returning from his conversation with the* ADMIRAL]. Well, Miss Kimbrough! I gather that you are already in some small measure rewarded!

EMILY [*brightly, quickly getting up*]. Oh? Yes, sir?

PURSER. Yes, indeed! Hodges has just informed me. It seems that our stowaway was also a thief!

EMILY. My goodness!

PURSER. Apparently he had been into your own belongings! Very close to him in the water, my men discovered this! [*He holds up Emily's safety-pocket.*]

CORNELIA [*in the voice of doom*]. Emily! . . .

EMILY [*turning to* CORNELIA, *starting to cry again*]. Cornelia!

[*Together,* EMILY *and* CORNELIA *are collapsing to the floor as the curtain falls.*]

FAST CURTAIN

ACT TWO

Scene One

SCENE: *The cabin again. About ten days later, the night before the boat is to dock at Le Havre. Late evening. The cabin is somewhat dimmer than before, lighted only by a table lamp this time. A chair has been added, left of the up center door. The chaise longue has been reversed, so that it is placed at an angle with the head toward the up center door. The hassock is now by its foot. There are strains of orchestra music above, playing a waltz of 1923.*]

AT RISE OF CURTAIN: *The cabin is empty, the door to the corridor open. We hear several laughing voices in the corridor, enchanted by the moonlight night, and then* CORNELIA *strolls into the doorway, followed by* LEO. CORNELIA *leans against the door frame a moment, a deliberate picture in her long evening gown. She is in her glory, flushed with success at the concert above, and loving* LEO'S *attentiveness.*]

LEO. Gee, you were wonderful, Cornelia! I never knew you could recite.

CORNELIA [*making a charming peevish face, and strolling into the cabin*]. Oh, that's the principal reason I'm making this trip—to take acting lessons in Paris.

LEO [*following* CORNELIA *in, the door standing open*]. You sure were the best one on the whole program. Were you surprised when they called on you?

CORNELIA [*carefully reclining on the chaise longue*]. Oh, I knew they always have a program the night before the boat docks—but, of course, I never dreamt they'd call on me!

LEO. Think of it! And you walked right out in the middle of the ballroom and did Lady Macbeth—just like that!

CORNELIA [*knowingly*]. That was the sleepwalking scene.

44

LEO [*with sudden clarification*]. Oh, *I* see! Dick said you were walking that way because the boat was rocking.

CORNELIA [*her face falling*]. Well, goodness! What did he mean by that?

LEO [*hastily*]. Oh, he was *very* impressed! And I'm sure the leader of the band thought you simply *saved* his concert!

CORNELIA [*appeased*]. And *how* did you like the singer to-night?

LEO. You mean the little fat lady who sang the song about when she was a young lad before her beard was grey?

[LEO *and* CORNELIA *both laugh, heartily. Then* LEO *sobers, a little nervously.*]

LEO. Oh, Cornelia! . . .

CORNELIA [*batting her eyelashes*]. Yes?

LEO. Say, listen. Would you—uh—would you come up to Harvard in November—for the Thanksgiving Prom?

CORNELIA [*spontaneously*]. Oh, I'd *love*——[*Then she pulls herself back.*] Why—that is—if I'm free that week-end. I'll have to look it up in my book.

LEO. Gee, it'd be swell if you——

CORNELIA [*archly*]. Dear me, I never thought medical students *had* proms!

LEO. Why not?

CORNELIA. I don't know. It sounds so frivolous. I thought they just spent all their time poking at dead bodies on ironing boards.

LEO. What do you mean? Post-mortems?

CORNELIA. Yes. Things like that. But don't tell me about them! [*She now leans forward, with a woman's deep interest in a man's work.*] Is it exciting to be a doctor, Leo?

LEO [*flattered, becoming professional*]. Well, I suppose it is. When you're a *doctor*. But being a medical student is a lot of hard, tough work.

CORNELIA. But aren't you *fascinated*?

LEO. Well, the work in the clinic is interesting. Of course, we students just get the routine calls. You know—colds and broken arms. That sort of thing. [*He suddenly brightens up.*] Although last year, Dick and I *did* get one swell case of cirrhosis of the liver. They took it away from us, but, while we had it, it was a beaut! [*He warms up tremendously.*] You see, this fellow came in——

CORNELIA [*rising quickly and strolling away*]. My, it *does* sound interesting, doesn't it?

[CORNELIA *drapes herself at the porthole, very lovely.* LEO, *cut off, simply looks at her for a second.*]

LEO [*gulping*]. Cornelia——

CORNELIA [*turning toward him, softly*]. Yes, Leo?

LEO. I—I'd like to ask you something. It's very important to me——

CORNELIA [*in hushed tones*]. Yes, Leo?

LEO. You don't have to say "yes" now, if you don't want to. You can take as long as you want to think about it——

CORNELIA. Leo. I don't need time to *think*.

LEO. Maybe you will, Cornelia! You don't know what it is— yet.

CORNELIA. Well, Leo—what is it?

LEO. Well, you see, Cornelia—I'm the president of our fraternity at Harvard.

CORNELIA [*with a shade of doubt in her voice*]. Yes?

LEO. And—we have a fraternity mascot. It's a skeleton. And every year it gets christened all over again. The president of the fraternity gets to choose the name.

CORNELIA [*with more doubt*]. Yes? . . .

LEO. Well—could I?

CORNELIA. Could you what?

LEO. Call our skeleton "Cornelia"—after you?

CORNELIA [*turning away with an awful expression*]. Why— uh—sure, Leo. I don't see why not!

[*The moment is interrupted by scurrying footsteps in the corridor, and* EMILY *bursts in, up center, dragging* DICK *after her by the hand. He is out of breath from keeping up with her.*]

EMILY. Cornelia! Get your life preserver!

CORNELIA. For heaven's sake, Emily! Why?

LEO. What's the matter?

EMILY [*tugging her own life preserver out from under the bunk*]. We're posting to starboard!

CORNELIA. Posting to starboard? [*She turns to* LEO, *frantically.*] What does that mean?

LEO. I don't know.

DICK [*as* CORNELIA *turns to him, giving a big, hopeless shrug*]. Don't ask *me!*

CORNELIA. Emily! What does it mean?

EMILY. *I* don't know. But we were up on deck and I heard someone shout it to the first mate. And from the way he said it, you could tell it meant something serious!

DICK [*with great superiority, preventing* EMILY *from putting on her preserver*]. Emily, child! *Put* that thing away.

EMILY. But we're in a fog! It came up suddenly. You can't see your hand in front of the prow! And they're blowing horns!

DICK. I *told* you, Emily! They *always* blow those horns in a fog——

LEO. Sure. To keep other ships a safe distance away.

EMILY. But the boat keeps bounding up and down—up and down!

CORNELIA. Oh, Emily, for heaven's sakes! We're not going to sink *now.* The trip's almost over. We dock tomorrow!

EMILY. But don't you see? That would be the most tragic part of all! To be drowned in sight of dry land!

DICK. Ye gods!

EMILY. Oh, it's all right for you to be brave! You're a man!

CORNELIA. Well, look at me! *I'm* not——

EMILY. Very well, Cornelia Skinner. You can be nonchalant in the face of danger if you want to. I'm going up and see if our lifeboat is still there. [*She starts for the door.*]

CORNELIA. Emily! You won't be able to find it in the dark! And even if you do find it, what good will that do?

EMILY. Of course, I can find it! There's a sign in the hall that says our lifeboat is number six on the portside.

DICK. Emily, we're *not* going up on deck poking around in those boats!

EMILY [*proudly*]. Nobody has to come with me. I can work alone. But, Cornelia Skinner—when the warning comes to take to the boats and everybody's shouting and screaming about women and children first—you'll be very glad that *somebody* knows where our lifeboat is!

[*Looking very darkly at* CORNELIA, EMILY *turns and goes out, up center.*]

DICK [*hopelessly*]. Whither she goest, I go, also.

[DICK *follows* EMILY *out.*]

LEO. That Emily. She's a card, isn't she?

CORNELIA [*maternally*]. She's a dear child. I'm very fond of her. [*She speaks dreamily.*] Our last night out! Heartbreaking, isn't it?

LEO. It's been a lot of fun. And now it's nearly over——

CORNELIA [*the dreamy mood again*]. Yes. You feel as though something had snapped—and could never be recaptured.

LEO [*quickly*]. Of course, we'll see each other again. In Paris?

CORNELIA [*with remote sadness*]. Yes, but you're going to England, first. And it all seems—so far away——

LEO. I suppose this *is* good-bye for now. We'll all be so busy in the morning.

CORNELIA. Yes, Leo. I suppose it is. [*She doesn't look at him, but speaks softly.*] Good-bye, Leo.

LEO. Good-bye, Cornelia.

[*Suddenly,* LEO *leans over and kisses* CORNELIA, *most briefly on the cheek. Then he straightens up and quickly starts for the door. Just as he reaches it,* CORNELIA, *who has not turned to him, lets out a rather low, throaty sound.*]

CORNELIA. Oh. Oh, dear.

LEO [*turning back in the doorway, nervously*]. Cornelia. You didn't mind—did you?

[CORNELIA *suddenly rises, abruptly, and strides across the room, away from* LEO. *He edges back into the room, worried.*]

LEO. Did you?

CORNELIA [*after a pause, biting her lip*]. Why. Why did I ever let you do it?

LEO [*with great concern*]. Oh, Cornelia! I'm terribly sorry! I—I never dreamt for one minute that such a *little* kiss——

CORNELIA [*not wanting to hear about how little it was, speaking over her shoulder*]. Oh, don't blame yourself. Don't. I'm just afraid now—that it's true.

LEO. What's true?

CORNELIA. What I've always known. Or at least—suspected.

LEO [*in anguish*]. *What,* Cornelia?

CORNELIA. That at heart, I'm—really a Magdalen.

LEO. Oh, Cornelia! You're not! You're *not* a Magdalen!

CORNELIA. Please, Leo. Don't say any more.

LEO. But I——

CORNELIA. It's my fault—all my fault—if you've lost respect for me.

LEO. But I haven't! I respect you very much!

CORNELIA [*with a hollow smile*]. Come now, Leo. We know better. If I've become—just a plaything, why——

LEO. Cornelia! The things you say!

CORNELIA. —why, then, I've only myself to blame.

LEO. But *I* kissed *you!*

CORNELIA. Yes, Leo. It's good of you to put it that way. But——

LEO. But what?

CORNELIA. Well, after all—a woman can foresee these things—and prepare for them.

LEO [*thunderstruck*]. You mean you *knew* I would?

CORNELIA [*womanly, with a pitying smile*]. Of course, Leo. You lamb!

LEO. Well, it's more than I knew myself!

CORNELIA. It's done, Leo. I'm sorry it had to end this way——

[*There are footsteps in the corridor, and* EMILY'S *and* DICK'S *voices are heard.*]

EMILY [*in the corridor*]. Thank you for coming with me, Dick!

DICK [*in the corridor*]. Don't mention it. I'll get the use of my legs back in a week or so. If we sink during the night, let me be the first to know, will you?

EMILY [*in the doorway, looking out*]. Good night, Dick.

DICK [*off*]. Night!

[*We hear* DICK'S *door slam, and* EMILY *turns into the room.* LEO *and* CORNELIA *have stopped to listen.* LEO *is a bit re-relieved at the interruption.*]

EMILY. There! I feel much better.

LEO. Oh! Did you find the lifeboat?

EMILY. Well, we found two of them.

CORNELIA. Two?

EMILY. Yes. I couldn't be sure which was the portside in the dark and with the boat moving—so I put cookies in both of them.

LEO *and* CORNELIA [*together*]. Cookies?

EMILY. Tinned biscuits would have been better. But I couldn't get any.

[EMILY *opens a small valise near the bunks.*]

CORNELIA. Well, I can just see us out on the open seas with a couple of fig newtons!

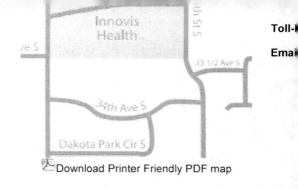

Download Printer Friendly PDF map

- **From the North:**

  - Take I-29 South to Exit 62
  - Turn Left onto 32nd Ave S
  - Go East approximately 6 blocks
  - Turn Left at 32nd Center strip mall. Large Hospital (Innovis

- **From the South:**

  - Take I-29 North to Exit 62
  - Turn Right onto 32nd Ave S
  - Go East approximately 6 blocks
  - Turn Left at 32nd Center strip mall. Large Hospital(Innovis

- **From the East:**

  - Take I-94 to I-29 south
  - Continue on I-29 south to Exit 62
  - Turn Left onto 32nd Ave S
  - Go East approximately 6 blocks
  - Turn Left at 32nd Center strip mall. Large Hospital (Innovis

EMILY [*at the valise, over her shoulder*]. Well, it will be better than raw fish—or sea gulls!

CORNELIA [*remembering the situation with* LEO, *turning to him now*]. Leo, you'd better go now. It's very late.

LEO [*heading for the door, and he'd just as soon*]. Oh, sure! Well . . .

[LEO *hesitates in the doorway, feeling he should say something more to* CORNELIA, *but she just motions him, rather tragically, to be silent. He swallows, and turns to* EMILY.]

LEO. Well, good night, Emily.

EMILY. Good night, Leo!

LEO [*earnestly, concerned*]. Good night, Cornelia! . . .

[CORNELIA *closes the door on* LEO, *as though putting him away from her.* EMILY, *meantime, has her nightgown out of the valise and is heading for the bathroom.*]

EMILY. Gee, I bet if this boat sank, there'd be lots of flotsam and jetsam!

CORNELIA [*now that the door is safely shut, practically jumping at* EMILY, *grabbing her wrist*]. Emily! Stop talking and listen!

EMILY. What?

CORNELIA [*dragging* EMILY *down to the chaise longue*]. Wait'll I *tell* you!

EMILY. Well—*what!*

CORNELIA [*screaming happily*]. Leo kissed me!

EMILY [*with a spontaneous squeal of delight*]. Cornelia! How did it happen?

CORNELIA [*with rapid excitement*]. Well, I'm a little vague about that. You know how it is when you're swept with a powerful emotion. Things become rather fuzzy—in your mind.

EMILY. Hm? Oh, sure, sure! [*She doesn't, but can't say so.*] But don't you *remember* anything about it?

CORNELIA [*after a slight pause, then adopting another mood*]. Dimly. Just very dimly. But as I recall—we were standing over there, near the table—and he was holding onto my fingers, as if he would never let them go. And then, suddenly, he turned away.

[EMILY *takes in a breath.*]

CORNELIA. The next thing I knew, I heard a choking sound. Like a strangled sob. And all at once I realized he was crying!

EMILY [*this merely confuses her*]. Crying? Well, for heaven's sakes, why?

CORNELIA [*testily*]. Well, why do you suppose, silly? Because he had to say good-bye to me!

EMILY. But he's going to see you again!

CORNELIA [*exasperated*]. Now, look, Emily—if you're going to take that tone, I won't tell you.

EMILY [*immediately acquiescent*]. Oh, no, please tell me! You heard him crying. Then what happened?

CORNELIA. Well, the next thing I knew—I was sitting here, and he had his head on my lap. And I was murmuring, "my dear, my dear." You know—like Candida with Marchbanks.

EMILY [*impatiently*]. Yes—but when did he kiss you?

CORNELIA. Just a minute. I'm coming to it. I was murmuring, "my dear, my dear," and then he jumped up. I could see he was once again master of himself. And then he clasped me to his breast and kissed me.

EMILY [*with a prolonged sigh*]. Oh! . . .

CORNELIA. The two of us—clinging together on an island in time. [*She speaks thrillingly.*] I was engulfed!

EMILY [*impressed*]. Was it really like that?

CORNELIA. I'm afraid I'm not very good at putting into words all that happened. [*She turns to* EMILY.] But surely you understand, Emily. Surely you've had some such experience. [*She means, of course, that she hasn't.*]

EMILY [*putting a face on it, weakly*]. Well, I played post office twice——

[EMILY *heads for the bathroom, arms over her shoulder, starting to undo her dress. She turns back at the door in this position.*]

EMILY. But I can't say that I was engulfed.

[*Thinking about it,* EMILY *turns and goes into the bathroom, leaving the door open.* CORNELIA *looks very satisfied. She starts to get her own nightgown out of her valise. After a moment, she calls out to* EMILY.]

CORNELIA. No, Emily. You've never felt a really *mature* emotion! Your idea of the male is some one who *builds,* and brings food *to,* the nest.

EMILY [*calling from inside the bathroom*]. What I don't see, Cornelia, is why you two made such a big fuss over it! When you're going to see each other in two weeks!

CORNELIA. You *are* a child, Emily. You can't realize. This thing is bigger than me. Bigger than him. Bigger than both of us.

EMILY [*in the bathroom*]. I don't know how it got all that big in just one week.

[*A sound of a foghorn is heard, above.*]

EMILY [*in the bathroom*]. Cornelia! There's that horn again! Oh, if I'd only learned to swim!

CORNELIA. Well, how did you ever get out of the Freshman class without learning? They don't let anybody out who can't swim the length of the pool in fifty strokes!

EMILY [*still in the bathroom*]. Oh, I learned to do that! But that's all. Fifty strokes. I can't do a single stroke more. And I can't even do that many if I don't count. And when I get nervous, I *can't* count! And I'd *certainly* be nervous if the boat was sinking! So I wouldn't be able to count, so I wouldn't be able to swim, so I'd drown. See?

[EMILY *appears from the bathroom in her nightgown, tying the belt.*]

CORNELIA [*heading for the bathroom with her nightgown*]. The only thing I see is that you'd better learn to count.

[CORNELIA *goes into the bathroom, where she is heard as the scene continues.*]

EMILY. Well, *I'm* nervous!

[EMILY *considers for a moment. Then, with* CORNELIA *out of the room, she suddenly gets an idea, moves a table out of the way to give her floor room, and then lies flat on her stomach on the floor and proceeds to do swimming strokes, meanwhile counting the strokes to herself.*]

CORNELIA [*calling out at about six*]. Emily! What are you doing?

EMILY. Never you mind! Better safe than sorry. [*She goes at it with renewed vigor, but only for a moment. Suddenly, she stops, thinking. She calls out to* CORNELIA.] Cornelia! Did you say—*engulfed?*

CORNELIA. *Uh-huh.* You know, Emily—I'm really *glad* Leo kissed me.

EMILY. Well, heavens! I always supposed you were.

CORNELIA. It actually will be helpful.

EMILY. Helpful? How?

CORNELIA. With my acting. You can't do the *great* parts until you've experienced real passion.

EMILY. Well, I thought you were wonderful as Lady Macbeth tonight, and that was *before* Leo kissed you.

CORNELIA. Oh, but that wasn't real acting, Emily. I was only falling back on my technique.

[CORNELIA *comes out of the bathroom in her nightgown.*]

CORNELIA. Emily, look. Who's going to sleep up tonight?

EMILY [*going right to the bunks and starting up*]. Oh, I don't mind. I'm lighter.

CORNELIA. Well, now, you're not *that* much lighter!

EMILY [*clambering into the top bunk*]. It's the bone structure. More delicate.

CORNELIA [*at the light switch*]. Are you in?

EMILY. Yes.

[CORNELIA *snaps off the lights. Only streaks of blue through the portholes very dimly light the room.*]

EMILY. Don't fall over anything in the dark.

CORNELIA [*groping for her bunk*]. No. I'm in. Good night, Emily.

EMILY. Good night, Cornelia.

[*There is a slight pause. Then two blasts from the forghorn— answered by a shrill whistle—are heard above.* EMILY *sits bolt upright in the dark.*]

EMILY. Cornelia! What was that?

CORNELIA. Oh, just those horns again.

EMILY [*already clambering down*]. But that was three blasts! That's dangerous!

CORNELIA. Emily! You're *not* coming down?

EMILY. I think I'd better check these portholes.

CORNELIA. Ye gods!

EMILY [*at the porthole*]. Cornelia! I'm afraid they're beginning to give under the strain.

CORNELIA [*still in bed*]. Them and me both! Emily—dear, sweet Emily, *will* you come back to bed!

EMILY [*as she does*]. Oh, very well. I'm going back up. You go to sleep.

CORNELIA. All right. You, too.

EMILY [*having settled herself in bed*]. Good night, Cornelia.

CORNELIA. Good night, Emily.

[*There is a pause, and then* EMILY *gets another notion.*]

EMILY. Cornelia?

CORNELIA [*sleepier*]. Hm?

EMILY. Do you hear a drip?

CORNELIA. A what?

EMILY. A drip. Close by.

CORNELIA [*angry*]. No, I *don't* hear a drip!

EMILY. I wonder if they've warned any of the passengers? [*She is starting down again.*]

CORNELIA [*with a groan of despair*]. Oh, Emily! [*Then she speaks with a sharp cry.*] Emily! Get your foot off my face!

EMILY. Oh, sorry, dear! It felt firm. [*She is down now and is crossing to the door, up center.*]

CORNELIA. It'll never be firm again!

EMILY. Well, why do you sleep with your face so far out? [*She opens the door and peers out. Then she closes it.*] No. Everything seems to be shipshape.

CORNELIA. Good!

EMILY [*going back and clambering up*]. Just so long as we're prepared. [*She has gotten settled once more.*] Good night, Cornelia.

CORNELIA. Good night, Emily!

[*There is a pause. Then a blowing sound comes from the top bunk.*]

CORNELIA [*groaning*]. *Now*, what are you doing?

EMILY. I'm blowing up my water wings.

CORNELIA. What's the matter with the life preserver?

EMILY. It's just so complicated to get on. I can manage the water wings. [*She settles down once again.*] Good night, Cornelia.

CORNELIA [*desperately*]. Good night, Emily.

[*There is a pause. Then* EMILY *speaks.*]

EMILY. Oh, Cornelia.

CORNELIA. *What?*

EMILY. All of a sudden I feel terribly peculiar.

CORNELIA [*with furious sarcasm*]. As if you were drowning, I bet!

EMILY. No. As if I was getting seasick.

CORNELIA [*shouting furiously*]. Emily! You've been on this boat ten days and you never got seasick!

EMILY [*queasily*]. All I know is how I feel.

CORNELIA [*with sudden decisiveness, getting out of bed herself*]. Emily! Come down out of there!

EMILY. Huh?

CORNELIA. I said, come down out of there!

EMILY [*doing so*]. Why, Cornelia?

CORNELIA [*climbing to the top bunk*]. If you're going to be seasick, I'm going to sleep up!

CURTAIN

ACT TWO

Scene Two

SCENE: *The cabin. Early the next morning. The hassock is over by the table, down right. The chaise longue is again turned. This time it is placed so that it runs up- and downstage, with the head toward the upright corner of the cabin.*]

AT RISE OF CURTAIN: CORNELIA *is still in bed. She tosses once or twice, rather feverishly, and then begins to sit up. There are whistles and banging sounds from above. In a second,* EMILY *emerges from the bathroom, looking very fresh, and straightening a bright new dress which she has just put on. She takes her nightgown to her already packed valise.*]

EMILY. Well, it's high time you woke up! We dock in half an hour.

[EMILY *sings "Frère Jacques" brightly and goes back to the bathroom.* CORNELIA *rises, starts down, staggers suddenly, and turns green. She clutches the post of the bunk for support and calls toward the bathroom.*]

CORNELIA. Oh, Emily——

EMILY. What?

CORNELIA. I'm sick.

EMILY [*running out of the bathroom*]. Cornelia! You *can't* be sick! Not today!

CORNELIA. I am. I am. I've got diphtheria, or something.

EMILY [*at* CORNELIA'S *side, concerned now*]. Cornelia, you *do* look pale! When did you start to feel it?

CORNELIA. Las' night. I got hot, and sort of feverish——

EMILY. Oh, Cornelia! Why didn't you call me?

CORNELIA. I thought—maybe—it was love.

EMILY. Oh.

CORNELIA. But it wasn't. It was a germ. I feel *awful!*

58

EMILY [*jumping up*]. The ship's doctor! I'll go get him!

CORNELIA. Tell him it feels like malaria—or yellow fever.

EMILY [*starting for the door, up center*]. Oh, I will! Right away, Cornelia!

[*Just as* EMILY *reaches the door, there is a knock on it. She starts, and then quickly opens it. It is the* STEWARD.]

EMILY. Yes?

STEWARD. Valises ready in five minutes, please!

EMILY. Oh, all right. Oh! Can you tell me where I have to go to find——

STEWARD. Sorry. All passengers are requested to remain in their cabins until the medical inspection is completed.

EMILY [*taken aback*]. Medical inspection?

STEWARD. That's right, miss. The Inspector will be aboard any minute. Stand by.

[*The* STEWARD *goes out, up center, closing the door.* EMILY *backs in a few steps, stunned, and closes the door.*]

CORNELIA. Emily—Emily—why don't you go? Don't leave me on this bed of pain.

EMILY [*horror-struck*]. Cornelia! I just thought!

CORNELIA. Don't think. Get the doctor.

EMILY. I can't. We *can't* get the doctor.

CORNELIA [*groaning*]. Why not?

EMILY. Because the boat lands today!

CORNELIA. I know the boat lands today! What of it?

EMILY. What the Steward said. Medical inspection! If I got the Doctor—and he says you're sick—they won't let you land. You'll be quarantined!

CORNELIA [*propping herself up, startled*]. What?

EMILY. Yes! They make you stay on board till you're well! The French Government is opposed to disease!

CORNELIA. Oh, no!

EMILY. They might even quarantine the whole boat!

CORNELIA [*desperately*]. How do you know?

EMILY. That's why they have this inspection. Aunt Alice got trapped in it once. Not exactly Aunt Alice. Her dog. He had the mange.

CORNELIA [*falling back*]. What I've got is worse than the mange.

EMILY [*wringing her hands*]. Oh, I wish I knew what to do!

CORNELIA. That's all right. You can't call the doctor. Just leave me here to die. They can wrap me in a sail and bury me at sea.

EMILY [*suddenly*]. I know!

CORNELIA. What?

EMILY. Leo—and Dick!

CORNELIA. What do you mean? That we'll be quarantined with them? I'm not up to it.

EMILY. No! Don't you see? They're *doctors!*

CORNELIA. Huh?

EMILY. Well, at least they will be when the graduate! They'll fix you up!

CORNELIA. But—but—they've only taken half the course——

EMILY. At least they can tell what's the matter with you! [*She starts for the door.*]

CORNELIA [*propping herself up, desperately*]. No—Emily, no! You can't tell them!

EMILY. Why not?

CORNELIA [*struggling into a sitting position*]. Emily—haven't you any sense of the fitness of things? Do you suppose after my big scene with Leo last night—I could face him—looking like this?

EMILY. Don't be silly!

CORNELIA. No, Emily! You simply *can't* stick out your tongue and say "ah" to a man you've just kissed!

EMILY. Well, you're going to, Cornelia Skinner. That's all there is to it! [*She opens the door, up center.*] I can't let you die!

CORNELIA. Emily—please——

[EMILY *is gone.* CORNELIA *groans.*]

CORNELIA. Oh, I'll bet I look gruesome.

[CORNELIA *struggles to her feet, across into the bathroom, and looks at herself in a mirror, as we hear* EMILY *knocking at the cabin down the hall.* CORNELIA *returns immediately from the bathroom.*]

CORNELIA. I do. I *do* look gruesome!

[*The* STEWARDESS *has come along the corridor and starts to come in the door, up center, as* CORNELIA *is struggling into a bathrobe.*]

STEWARDESS Stewardess, miss. May I come in yet?

CORNELIA [*turning away to hide her appearance, supporting herself on the bunk*]. No. No, please. Some other time. Next summer, maybe——

[CORNELIA *is waving the* STEWARDESS *away with her hand. She looks puzzled, and starts to back out into the corridor.*]

STEWARDESS. Be sure you don't leave anything, miss. That's why I'm checking up.

[*As the* STEWARDESS *backs into the corridor,* EMILY *and* LEO *appear, bustling past her, and shutting the door on her.* LEO *carries a small kit, and goes right to* CORNELIA.]

LEO. Cornelia! Emily says you're sick.

CORNELIA [*trying to be brave*]. Yes. Isn't it ridiculous?

LEO [*leading her to a chair*]. Here. Sit down while I look at you.

CORNELIA. And I'm such a healthy girl, too. Emily, wasn't I voted the healthiest girl in the class, or something?

[CORNELIA *looks about vaguely, letting* LEO *seat her and feel her pulse.*]

EMILY. Don't talk, Cornelia. That encourages the germs. I'll pack your things.

[EMILY *grabs* CORNELIA'S *valise and begins flinging things into it.*]

LEO. Stick out your tongue. You don't have to say "ah."

EMILY. I told him you most expressly didn't want to say "ah." [*She is folding one of* CORNELIA'S *dresses.*] But *should* I pack? What if we have to stay here?

LEO. Emily. Come here a minute.

EMILY [*rushing over to* LEO, *worried*]. Can I help? A tourniquet, or something?

LEO. Look at her closely. Do those look like spots to you?

EMILY [*peering at* CORNELIA'S *face*]. Why, they most definitely *do* look like spots! What is it—spotted fever?

LEO. Cornelia. Have you ever had the measles?

CORNELIA [*aghast*]. Measles! Why, no!

EMILY. She hasn't got—*measles?*

CORNELIA. I couldn't have measles! Only kids get measles!

LEO. No. Adults can get them, too. In fact, it's more serious.

CORNELIA. Oh, *no!*

[*The door, up center, opens and* DICK *hurries in, just getting his tie on.*]

DICK. What is it? What's the matter with her?

LEO. I've got an idea. See what you think.

CORNELIA. Yeah, come and see the spotted wonder. Twenty-five cents a look.

[DICK *goes to* CORNELIA, *who is on the chaise longue, and repeats the examination while the others wait suspensefully for his words.*]

DICK [*looking at* LEO]. Measles?

LEO. That's what I think.

DICK. Not much doubt about it. And a beaut of a case!

EMILY [*with great sympathy*]. Oh, Cornelia!

CORNELIA. Well, that's just great! [*She starts to bawl, in spite of herself.*] And when the boat docks in a few minutes, *I* won't! I'll be quarantined! My whole vacation!

EMILY. I'll stay with you, Cornelia! I've already had the measles. And I can see France some other time!

CORNELIA [*crying*]. No—no—I can't let you sacrifice yourself.

LEO [*exchanging glances with* DICK]. They might quarantine us, too.

EMILY. I'll read to you, Cornelia. They have a lot of novels by Thackeray up in the library.

CORNELIA [*with a wail*]. Oh!

DICK [*meaningfully, to* LEO]. Of course, the spots won't be really bad for twenty-four hours.

LEO [*significantly*]. That's what I was thinking.

EMILY [*helpfully*]. You hear that, Cornelia? That's nice, isn't it?

CORNELIA. Oh, sure. Sure. I have something to look forward to.

DICK [*carrying on an implied conversation with* LEO]. How do you think she looks—now?

LEO [*looking her over*]. Well, not too good. But——

CORNELIA. You don't have to spare me. I look ghastly!

DICK [*with raised eyebrows, to* LEO]. Do you think it might work?

LEO. Maybe. We could try.

EMILY [*realizing that something is going over her head*]. What are you two talking about, anyway?

DICK. Look. Does anyone else know about this?

LEO. The Steward, or anybody?

EMILY. No-o, I don't think so. Why?

DICK. Then we've got a chance!

EMILY. A chance at what?

LEO. Keeping it from everybody.

CORNELIA. What for?

EMILY. What are you going to do?

DICK. Smuggle her out.

EMILY. *Smuggle?*

CORNELIA. You make me feel like a box of opium.

LEO. If we can get you past the health inspector—that's the main thing.

DICK. Of course, we'll have to write a letter back to the ship and tell them. So they can fumigate this cabin.

EMILY. Yes! Otherwise, you might start an epidemic!

CORNELIA. Just call me Typhoid Mary.

DICK. Now, listen. I'll go up to the infirmary and see if I can get some medicine without arousing their suspicions.

LEO. Cornelia—you've got to get dressed somehow——

CORNELIA. I couldn't! I can't stand up!

DICK [*to* EMILY]. Well, can't you put some things on her, over that nightgown? Cover it up?

EMILY. Oh, sure! I'll think of something! [*She casts her eyes around the room feverishly for clothing.*]

LEO. She's *got* to cover those spots! That's a dead giveaway!

CORNELIA [*getting interested now, in spite of the way she feels*]. Well, I *am* good at make-up. My theatre background——

LEO. Who'll inspect them, Dick?

DICK. The French Government sends somebody out on a tender. [*He starts for the door.*] And don't let anybody in here to see her—till we get back!

[DICK *hurries out, up center.*]

LEO [*in the doorway, as* DICK *goes*]. Don't worry, Cornelia. We'll stand by you till the end.

CORNELIA. I have a feeling that'll be any minute now.

[LEO *follows* DICK *out, quickly, closing the door.*]

EMILY [*swinging into action*]. Now, don't be despondent. Cornelia. [*She brings* CORNELIA *a vanity case.*] Put lots of powder on your face. You can just wear your coat over that bathrobe!

CORNELIA [*dabbing white powder furiously all over her face*]. Oh, dear!

EMILY [*just as furiously packing what is left for their two valises*]. If we can just get you off the boat, Cornelia! You can *recuperate* in France!

CORNELIA [*still dabbing*]. I didn't come to France to recuperate! I came to learn acting and to see Paris!

EMILY. Well, you can see *part* of Paris from a hotel room. The Eiffel Tower sticks way up!

CORNELIA. I may not even recuperate. I'm an adult! It would be just my luck to die of the measles. How humiliating!

EMILY [*finishing the valises and putting them near the door*]. I've got the bags packed! How do you look?

[CORNELIA *turns to* EMILY, *dead white with the powder.*]

EMILY. Well, you certainly can't see the spots.

CORNELIA. I look as if I'd been ducking for apples in a paper-hanger's bucket!

EMILY [*critically*]. We-l-l—it may be just a little *too* white, Cornelia. I know! Put lots of lipstick on! That'll *distract* them!

CORNELIA [*taking a lipstick*]. Yes, and they'll think I'm traveling with the Ringling Brothers' Circus!

[*There is a knock at the door. It is the* STEWARD.]

STEWARD [*offstage*]. Bags, miss?

EMILY [*handing the valises to the* STEWARD *in the corridor*]. Oh, all right. Coming right out.

STEWARD. Yes, miss. Thank you, miss.

CORNELIA [*as* EMILY *closes the door, breaking down*]. Emily, I can't do it! I can't get ready! I'm going to give myself up!

EMILY. Not now, Cornelia. Not now! We're halfway there! [*She snatches up* CORNELIA'S *coat.*] Here. Let me help you get your coat on. No one must know you're in a bathrobe!

CORNELIA [*halfway up, supporting herself as* EMILY *slips the coat on her*]. I can't stand up, Emily! I can't!

EMILY. It's all right. You can be seated when the Inspector comes. [*She is happy now.*] Just think! We're going to be eating French fried potatoes in France! [*She buttons the coat, and notices the lipstick now for the first time.*] Oh, I think the lipstick does the job all right!

CORNELIA. I made it bigger than my mouth. To *distract*.

EMILY [*stepping back, critically*]. Still, it looks sort of weird. [*She quickly glances about the room.*] Here! Put this on! [*She snatches a very large hat with a veil.*]

CORNELIA. But that's *wild*. It doesn't go with this coat!

EMILY [*putting it on* CORNELIA's *head*]. It's got a veil, though. We'll pull it down over your eyes so they can't see how dazed you look! [*She hums as she fastens the hat and lowers the veil.*] "Frère Jacques—frère Jacques—dormez-vous——"

CORNELIA. Emily! Don't sing. Above all, don't sing in French!

EMILY. There! You practically can't see *you* at all!

[*The door, up center, opens and* DICK *slips in, a bottle in his hand.*]

DICK. How is she?

EMILY [*cheerfully*]. Oh, we're coming right along!

DICK. I got something. I'll get a glass in the bathroom. [*He goes quickly into the bathroom and the sound of tap water running is heard.*]

EMILY [*suddenly*]. Oh! I just got another idea! I'll be right back!

[EMILY *runs to the door, up center, and out, down the corridor.*]

DICK [*returning from the bathroom*]. Here, now, drink this. It's nothing but a nerve tonic, but it'll keep you on your feet.

CORNELIA [*taking the glass, lifting it with great distaste*]. "Come, vial, my dismal scene I needs must act alone. Romeo, this do I drink to thee." [*She pours it down in one gulp, and then chokes and sputters.*]

DICK. There, now! It's not so bad, is it?

CORNELIA. No. For hemlock, it's really rather tasty.

[EMILY *slips in from the corridor, carrying something wrapped in her hand.*]

EMILY. Oh, fine! Did you give it to her?

DICK [*nodding*]. She'll be all right.

CORNELIA [*trying to rise*]. Oh, Lemly—I feel shuddenly sho dizshy——

EMILY [*pushing CORNELIA back*]. Cornelia, don't! Just sit back. Be calm. Oh, the rash is beginning to show through. You need more white powder!

[EMILY *grabs the powder puff and starts in again.* CORNELIA *avoids it. She is sick.*]

CORNELIA. No—no—it musht be the medishine—I've got to lie down——

[LEO *slips in at the door, up center.*]

LEO. The Inspector's doing this corridor now! She'll be here any minute!

DICK. Cornelia! You *can't* lie down!

EMILY. Cornelia! Here's something else! [*She unwraps what she has brought in. It is a very large piece of chocolate cake.*] Eat this!

CORNELIA [*with great revulsion*]. Oh! Take it away!

EMILY. No! Don't you see? It's a brilliant idea! When the inspector comes, you're eating this cake! It'll practically hide the bottom of your face, and the veil takes care of the top! See?

[EMILY *forces the cake on* CORNELIA.]

CORNELIA. This is the end! This is all I needed!

[*There is a sharp knock on the door.*]

DICK. There's the Inspector!

LEO. Cornelia—can you do it?

EMILY. Don't say anything. Just nod!

[CORNELIA *nods blearily*. DICK *and* LEO *come to attention.* EMILY *runs to the door, up center. She takes a deep breath and opens it. Outside, stands the* ADMIRAL, *a large loving cup in his hand.*]

ADMIRAL [*coming right in*]. Miss Kimbrough! What great pleasure it gives me to be able to pay you this visit!

[*There is a moan from* CORNELIA. *Everybody else is frantic.*]

EMILY. Oh—could we see you a little later—just now we're——

ADMIRAL [*with great good cheer*]. You certainly could not see me a little later! What—and miss this opportunity? Why, the boat's docking now!

[*Shrill whistles and shouts and band music are heard above.*]

ADMIRAL. There! You see? We're in. And, later, I should not have the great good fortune—[*He crosses to where* COR-NELIA *sits; everybody stiffens.*]—to present to Miss Skin-ner—with the compliments of the entire ship——[*He suddenly peers down.*] This *is* Miss Skinner, isn't it?

ALL [*quickly*]. Oh, yes—yes!

ADMIRAL [*a little disturbed by* CORNELIA'S *appearance, but pulling himself together*]. Ah—to present Miss Skinner with a little memento of her splendid performance at last night's concert. She has been voted the finest performer by the entire crew, and, in consequence, this loving cup is offered in humble token of our esteem. [*He gives* CORNELIA *the cup, which she simply stares into, blankly, as he bows low.*] Miss Skinner.

EMILY [*taking command of the situation, and also taking him by the arm, quickly*]. Why, Mr. Hodges, thank you! Oh, Cornelia is *so* pleased! Aren't you, Cornelia? [*This is called out over her shoulder, as she is ushering the* ADMIRAL *to the door, to his considerable perplexity.*] She'll treasure this always, Mr. Hodges. And be assured she'll never forget this moment. [*She practically pushes him out the door.*] Thank you, Mr. Hodges. And thank you again!

[EMILY *shuts the door on the* ADMIRAL. CORNELIA *bursts into a loud sob.*]

EMILY. Cornelia, hush!

[ALL *start to* CORNELIA *to comfort her, but there is an immediate rap on the door.* ALL *freeze. It is the* INSPECTOR, *who has a French accent.*]

INSPECTOR [*offstage*]. Health inspection!

EMILY [*after a second's terror for* ALL]. Oh, yes. Yes, come in.

[EMILY *crosses to the door, up center, and brings the* INSPECTOR *downstage, being very careful to keep her away from* CORNELIA, *who is being covered by* DICK *and* LEO.]

EMILY. I'm Emily Kimbrough. What did you want to know?

INSPECTOR [*writing on a pad*]. Emily Kimbrough . . . you share this cabin with someone?

EMILY. Oh, yes! Indeed. Her! [*She points to* CORNELIA, *smiling.*]

INSPECTOR [*taking a step toward* CORNELIA, *as* ALL *become uneasier*]. Name, please?

CORNELIA [*taking the cake out of her mouth, speaking through a fog*]. Corne'a Skinner——

INSPECTOR [*looking up sharply*]. What's that again, please?

EMILY. Cornelia Skinner—that's her name!

DICK [*reassuring the* INSPECTOR]. Yes—Skinner.

LEO [*helping too much*]. Cornelia *Otis* Skinner.

INSPECTOR [*writing*]. Ages?

EMILY. Nineteen. Going on twenty.

INSPECTOR [*to* CORNELIA, *with an especial eye for her now*]. You, too?

[CORNELIA *just makes a gurgling sound, nodding vehemently, and chewing and chewing on the cake. The general effect is somewhat that of a moron.*]

INSPECTOR. Ever been in France before?

EMILY [*trying to get between* CORNELIA *and the* INSPECTOR].
Oh, no! The very first time. I love it, though!

INSPECTOR [*to* CORNELIA, *circling around* EMILY]. What about
you?

[CORNELIA *simply sways her head from side to side, rythmic-
ally, to indicate "no." The* INSPECTOR *is frowning at her by
now.*]

INSPECTOR. Are you both in good health?

EMILY. Oh, yes. Yes, fine!

[*The* INSPECTOR *glances at* CORNELIA.]

CORNELIA [*trying too enthusiastically*]. Oh, yes! Yes—fine!
[*She has switched from shaking her head "no" to nodding
"yes," without actually stopping the movement of her head.*]
Thertingly.

[*The* INSPECTOR *shoots her a sharp glance. That was a bit too
much.* EMILY *leaps to the rescue.*]

EMILY. Cornelia! I told you not to eat any more of that cake!
The Inspector can't understand a word you're saying! [*She
gets down between the* INSPECTOR *and* CORNELIA, *trying to
be bright.*] She's eaten almost the whole cake, and a piece of
pie, just this morning. Such a zesty appetite!

INSPECTOR [*dubiously*]. I see. Well—that is all. . . .

[*As the* INSPECTOR *turns toward the door, with* ALL *hopefully
on needles and pins, the door, up center, opens and* HARRIET
and WINIFRED *breeze in, and head for the cabinet.*]

HARRIET. Would you think it of me? Left the dentifrice again!

WINIFRED. Oh, sorry, Inspector! Didn't know you were here.
Come another time.

HARRIET [*having picked up her toothpaste*]. Got it, anyway.
[*On her way out, she notices* CORNELIA, *and stops.*] Why,
my dear girl! Whatever in the world is wrong?

WINIFRED. You look simply fearful!

[The OTHERS *just about have heart failure, but* EMILY *comes to the rescue.]*

EMILY. Well, I like that! Just because you've never liked that hat on Cornelia! *[She gets them to the door.]* I must say you're very rude, you two!

HARRIET. Oh, I say, now! . . .

[But EMILY *has got them out, shutting the door. The* INSPECTOR *starts for the door.]*

EMILY *[to the* INSPECTOR, *trying to smile].* They feel Americans dress so poorly.

INSPECTOR *[at the door, considering].* I see. Miss Kimbrough, would you mind stepping outside with me? *[She gives a dubious glance back at* CORNELIA.] I'd like to have a word with you.

EMILY *[dismay all over her face].* Why—why, no—not at all— that is——

[The INSPECTOR *and* EMILY *go out, up center, shutting the door.* LEO *and* DICK *clasp their hands to their foreheads, sunk.* CORNELIA *groans.]*

DICK. That does it!

LEO. She caught on!

DICK. Oh, lord!

CORNELIA *[starting to wail].* And you two! You're implicated!

LEO. Yeah, but we're not sick——

CORNELIA. But you're medical students! You'll be disbarred— or defrocked—or something!

LEO *[going white].* Say, Dick! Do you think they might?

DICK. It'd better not get back to Harvard, that's all I've got to say!

CORNELIA. And it's all my fault!

*[CORNELIA *goes into sobs.* LEO *and* DICK *rush to her, comforting her.]*

LEO. Oh, now, Cornelia! We'd have done it for *anybody!*

DICK. Don't upset yourself. You'll make it worse!

[EMILY *comes back in, alone, closing the door.* ALL *turn to her, tense.*]

DICK. Well?

LEO. Are we sunk?

EMILY [*frowning*]. No—no, I don't think so.

DICK. What?

LEO. You don't mean she got by?

EMILY. Well, I don't think the Inspector thought Cornelia was *ill*——

DICK. Then what?

LEO. *Tell* us.

EMILY. Well—what she wondered is if Cornelia oughtn't to take a mental test.

CORNELIA [*with a scream*]. What!

EMILY. Yes. It seems they don't let you into the country if you haven't the mentality of a child seven years old.

CORNELIA [*collapsing back onto the chaise longue*]. Oh!

EMILY. But I told her you *must* have a mentality of seven years old because you've been two years to college!

LEO *and* DICK. Well?

EMILY. So—she said she guessed then it'd be all right.

DICK. You mean?

LEO. You mean we passed?

EMILY. Yes. I guess we did. Isn't that good!

[LEO *and* DICK *let out huge cries of relief and fall into chairs.* CORNELIA *has fainted dead away.*]

EMILY. Well, look! Don't just sit there! We're in dock!

DICK. That's right. We'd better get her up there.

LEO. Before anybody comes along!

DICK. Come on, Cornelia! Up we go!

[DICK *has taken one hand and* LEO *the other, but* CORNELIA *simply slumps forward, out.*]

LEO. Ye gods! She's fainted!

EMILY [*running around in front of* CORNELIA *and down on her knees*]. Oh, no! Cornelia! Don't do this to us! We passed the inspection. Just a little more effort and we'll make the deck. Then I'll get you in a cab, and we'll ride to a hotel, and——

DICK [*rubbing* CORNELIA'S *wrists*]. Cornelia! Cornelia! You've got to try!

CORNELIA [*coming to, vaguely*]. Huh? What happened?

EMILY. We're going up now, Cornelia! You've got to be brave!

LEO. You've got to stand on your feet!

[LEO *and* DICK *try to raise* CORNELIA.]

CORNELIA. Oh, no—I can't—I wobble——[*She is about to give in.*] Get the doctor!

DICK [*hopelessly*]. After *all* this?

EMILY [*with a look in her eye, a last chance*]. Cornelia. Look here. You want to act. Don't you?

[CORNELIA *bobs her heavy head "yes."*]

EMILY. You think you can. Don't you?

[CORNELIA *bobs again, a little better.*]

EMILY. Well, if you think you can, or if you ever want or hope to, you've got to prove it right now!

CORNELIA. Huh?

EMILY. Cornelia Skinner. You've got to act like a well woman!

CORNELIA. What? Act? Of course, I can.

EMILY. I *dare* you, Cornelia!

CORNELIA. Course I can. Out of my way!

[CORNELIA *flails her arms, as though about to do it alone.* LEO *and* DICK *duck, and* CORNELIA *nearly tumbles on her face. They grab her again, and start to walk, supporting her.*]

CORNELIA. You don't have to support me—I'm a well woman— I'm landing in France—I can hear the band——

[LEO *and* DICK *are steering* CORNELIA *to the door.*]

CORNELIA. Don't you hear the music, Emily?

[*There is band music above.*]

CORNELIA. What's the matter, Emily? Don't you feel well? Be of good cheer. Stout fella, now!

[*They have got her into the corridor and out of sight on the last phrase.* EMILY *darts back to the bunks and gathers up the powder and lipstick. Before she is through,* DICK *runs back into the room, terrified.*]

DICK. Emily! She's going to be sick, right now!
EMILY [*horrified*]. Oh! [*She tries desperately to think.*]
DICK [*with a groan*]. What are we going to do?
EMILY [*getting her idea*]. Have faith! Have faith!

[EMILY *darts to the chaise longue, picks up the loving cup, and hands it to* DICK. *He stares at it a moment, and then catches on. Both run out into the corridor in* CORNELIA'S *direction as the curtain falls.*]

CURTAIN

ACT THREE
Scene One

SCENE: *The interior of the hotel room in Paris. It is an old-fashioned room, in an inexpensive, shabby-genteel tradition. There is a door, up center, leading to the hallway, with a hallway backing beyond it leading only toward right stage. The hallway ends, going toward left, precisely at the door to this room. In the left upstage corner are two windows, as though the building had a jutting corner—one in the back wall and one in the left wall. Placed in this corner, and stretching down left against the left wall, is a cot. Below this, extreme downstage left, is a telephone table with a telephone of the period, and a lamp, and a chair nearby. In the upstage right corner, stretching against the back wall toward center, is a very old four-poster canopied bed.* In the right wall, about the center of it, is the door to the bathroom. An antiquated chair is upstage of this door. Below it, on the downstage right wall, is a large gilt-framed painting.]*

AT RISE OF CURTAIN: *The room is empty, although one of the girls' trunks is at center stage. Immediately, the door, up center, is opened by* THÉRÈSE, *a young French girl and daughter of the proprietress, who enters, carrying two valises and ushering* EMILY *and* CORNELIA *into the room.* THÉRÈSE *wears an apron and serves as general maid-of-all-work to her mother. She is dressed in a French costume of the early twenties, with a touch of the colorful peasant for the benefit of the tourist trade.* CORNELIA *and* EMILY *are in fresh outfits—suits—and* CORNELIA *is looking pretty fit again. It is a*

---

*This bed may be carried offstage right, as though into an alcove, if limited stage space demands.

little more than two weeks later. The girls are, of course, eye-ing everything thoroughly as they enter. THÉRÈSE *goes di-rectly to stage left, and deposits the valises just below the cot.*]

CORNELIA. Emily! Isn't it *quaint?*

EMILY. Yes. Do you think it's a villa or a château?

CORNELIA [*going toward the door in the right wall*]. I wonder what's in here. . . .

[CORNELIA *strolls off into the bathroom. Meantime,* THÉRÈSE *has returned to the up center door, about to leave.*]

THÉRÈSE. C'est tout, mademoiselle?

EMILY. Oh—ja! I mean, oui! C'est très joli. Merci bien!

[THÉRÈSE *grins and bobs and starts out.* EMILY *suddenly re-members and dives for the door, grabbing it.*]

EMILY. Oh, look—wait a minute! I mean—pardon, mais— [*Her French is labored.*]—est-ce—possible—pour—*us*— [*She gives up, starting over.*] I mean—nous desirons—faire—*un bath!*

[THÉRÈSE *frowns prettily, looking blank.*]

EMILY. Un laver! Rub, rub, rub.

[EMILY *furiously pantomimes scrubbing herself with a bath-brush. As the girl looks blanker,* CORNELIA *returns.*]

CORNELIA. Emily—what on earth are you doing?

EMILY. I'm simply trying to explain to this girl that we'd like to take a bath.

THÉRÈSE [*the light breaking immediately*]. Oh, the mademoi-selles would like to take a bath! Why did she not say so?

EMILY. Well! Why did you not tell me that you could speak English?

THÉRÈSE. I simply thought you would suppose it for granted.

EMILY. Oh! Well, yes—we would like to take a bath.

CORNELIA [*indicating the bathroom*]. There's a great big tub in there. I suppose it's a bathtub. Either that or they make illegal gin up here.

THÉRÈSE. Yes. It is a tub for the bath.

CORNELIA. Merci—I mean, thank you very much.

[THÉRÈSE *smiles prettily and starts to go.* EMILY *is taking off her hat.*]

EMILY. My—I'm hot after that train ride!

THÉRÈSE [*having almost gone, thinking of something*]. Oh, mademoiselle, I feel that I must warn you.

EMILY. Warn us? About what?

THÉRÈSE. About the water for the bath. There is a petite gas metre over the tub. Into which you put the centimes.

CORNELIA. Centimes? What for?

THÉRÈSE. To pay for the gas which heats the water.

EMILY [*as she and* CORNELIA *are satisfied*]. Oh. All right.

THÉRÈSE [*sweetly*]. That is where the danger lies.

EMILY [*immediately shaken again*]. Danger? What danger?

THÉRÈSE. Well—if it is that you are in the tub—and the metre —it starts clicking—then you must quickly put in another twenty-five centime—or she will explode.

CORNELIA. What will explode?

THÉRÈSE [*with a shrug*]. The whole thing.

EMILY [*wide-eyed*]. It would really *explode?*

THÉRÈSE [*giving it great consideration*]. About this we are not positive. But in the past month, two metres have explode. And we conclude that is the reason. People do not put in the centimes quick enough.

[CORNELIA *and* EMILY *look at each other in great fear.*]

EMILY [*aghast*]. Well, thank you very much for *telling* us!

THÉRÈSE [*matter-of-factly*]. Oh, you are most welcome.

[THÉRÈSE *goes out, up center, closing the door.*]

EMILY. Well, how do you like that? [*She starts to unpack.*]

CORNELIA [*also starting to unpack*]. Sounds like that old volcano that had to be fed two maidens every spring, or it erupted over the whole island.

EMILY [*pointing out of the window suddenly*]. Cornelia! Look! Isn't that—isn't that . . .

CORNELIA. Oh, Emily—it is! It really is!

EMILY [*both wrapt in admiration*]. The Eiffel Tower! Oh, Cornelia—isn't it *lovely?*

CORNELIA [*sighing, their arms around each other*]. Yes!

EMILY. Think of it! We're in Paris. And looking right out at the Eiffel Tower.

CORNELIA. Emily! Way down there, see? Past that little park. That must be the Arc de Triomphe.

EMILY [*quietly*]. When we were little and we heard about a dance or a picnic or anything exciting, the kids in Indiana used to say, "I hope I get to go." And now—I *did* get to go. I'm here. In Paris.

CORNELIA [*suddenly*]. Oh, good lord!

EMILY [*startled*]. What?

CORNELIA. I almost forgot! Oh, how terrible!

EMILY. What's terrible?

CORNELIA. I've been here a whole hour already—and I haven't called him.

EMILY. Called who?

CORNELIA. Monsieur de la Croix! Of the Comédie Française!

EMILY. Oh. Oh, sure. Well, there's the telephone. You can call him right away.

CORNELIA [*grabbing her purse*]. I've got the telephone number here somewhere. I had a porter get it for me in Le Havre. [*She takes out the slip of paper.*] Yes! [*She smooths it out in front of her, going to the telephone.*]

EMILY [*finishing her unpacking*]. Oh, I do hope he'll take you, Cornelia.

CORNELIA [*sitting at the telephone table, putting the slip of paper on it*]. Oh, he's got to. He's *got* to.

[CORNELIA *lifts the receiver to her ear, moistening her lips. She has become breathy and nervous. She holds the receiver suspended for a second, then suddenly puts it back on the hook and clenches her hands, staring front, breathing harder.*]

EMILY. Well, go ahead, Cornelia! What's holding you back?

CORNELIA [*between breaths*]. Now, wait—don't rush me. I've got to get myself composed. You just don't call up the greatest living French actor without thinking of what you're going to say!

EMILY. Cornelia Skinner, you've been thinking of what you were going to say for the last five weeks!

CORNELIA. Oh, all right. [*She turns to the telephone and puts out her hand to lift the receiver, but then jumps up.*] But wait'll I comb my hair.

EMILY. Comb your hair? For heaven's sake, he can't *see* you on the phone!

CORNELIA [*having gone to her purse and taken out a comb, running it through her hair*]. No—I know that—but I'll *feel* better. I won't be so nervous if my hair is combed.

EMILY [*in disgust, starting for the telephone*]. *I'll* call him.

CORNELIA [*diving after* EMILY, *pulling her away*]. No! Emily, wait! You might make the wrong impression!

EMILY [*offended*]. Well, I don't see why! Nobody asked *me* to take a mental test.

CORNELIA [*rubbing her hands at the telephone*]. Now, let's see. The number is——[*She has a change of heart.*] No. First, I've got to take my breathing exercises. [*She hurries back to the center of the room and lies down on the floor.*]

EMILY [*giving up*]. Oh, you four-flusher!

CORNELIA [*extending her arms and taking deep noisy breaths*]. If I don't—my voice will sound breathy—and terrible—and he'll think I'm hopeless—and he won't take me.

[CORNELIA *begins to make "oh" and "ah" sounds with each exhalation.* EMILY *gets up and crosses upstage of her.*]

EMILY. You silly! After all this, what if he's not even in?

CORNELIA [*continuing her exercises*]. Emily, you simply are incapable of realizing the importance of good chest tones. He could tell in a minute if I wasn't using my diaphragm. [*She sits up.*] There, now. I feel a little better. See? [*She rises and goes to the telephone.*] Emily, I'll tell you what. You can call the number. I'll let you.

EMILY [*going to the telephone, to get on with it*]. Thanks for the favor. [*She takes up the receiver.*]

CORNELIA. But I'll talk to him!

EMILY [*into the telephone, reading off the paper*]. Odeon, deux-quatre-six-un, please. . . . Merci. . . .

[*CORNELIA is fidgeting all over the place.*]

EMILY. Cornelia. Stop jumping around like that! [*She speaks back into the telephone.*] What? . . . Oh, no, not you. . . . What? . . . You're ringing it? [*She gets the number.*] Oh. Hello. May I please speak with Monsieur de la Croix, please. . . . De—la—Croix. . . . Yes. [*She turns to* CORNELIA.] They're getting him. Come on!

CORNELIA. Oh, Emily, I'm paralyzed! I don't think I can speak to him! Tell him—tell him I'm sick!

EMILY [*back into the telephone*]. Monsieur de la Croix? . . . Un moment, s'il vous plaît. [*She speaks in a hoarse whisper to* CORNELIA.] He doesn't even know who you are! How can I tell him you're sick? Here! [*She thrusts the telephone to* CORNELIA.] You've *got* to talk to him!

[EMILY *walks away, leaving* CORNELIA *with the telephone.*]

CORNELIA [*with considerable stage fright*]. Uh—hello! . . . What? . . . Oh, yes—I speak in the English. Do you? . . . Oh, how lovely! . . . What? . . . No, this isn't a joke. This is Cornelia Skinner. . . . Yes. Skinner. I'm an American. . . . No, I'm not calling from America. I'm right here in Paris. This minute! Aren't we, Emily? . . . [*She nods brightly, away from the telephone.*] What? . . . Oh, what

is it that I wish? Well, it is that I wish that—uh—would
you teach me acting, Mr. de la Croix, *would* you? Hm? . . .
[*Her face falls.*] You're awfully busy? Oh, but Mr. de la
Croix, I came all the way from—and I've just recovered from
the measles, too—I saw your picture in an American magazine, and—I told my father all about you——[*She suddenly
pauses to listen.*] Yes. Skinner. Cornelia *Otis* Skinner. . . .
Yes, he's my father. . . . What? . . . [*She cries with great
joy.*] Oh, Monsieur de la Croix, you *will?* . . . Oh, that's
wonderful! When? . . . Right away? . . . Fifteen minutes? Why—I guess—yes. You could inspect me in fifteen
minutes. We're at the Hotel San Sulpice. Sixteen Rue de
la——Oh, you know? You're right near here? . . . Well,
that's fine! . . . Yes. Thank you. . . . Yes, thank you. . . .
Yes. [*She puts down the receiver, dreamily, and starts toward
the bed.*]

EMILY. What is it? What did he say?

CORNELIA. He wants to inspect me.

EMILY. Oh, how good! I suppose you didn't feel you could ask
him—about taking me this first time?

CORNELIA. Oh, Emily, now—it wouldn't be a bit of help to your
dancing!

EMILY [*crushed at being left out*]. Oh, I just thought—it
might.

CORNELIA [*suddenly waking up, dashing for her clothes*]. He's
coming right away! I've got to change! I've got to dress!
Where are my things? Oh, everything's crushed! [*She feverishly gets a dress out of the valise.*]

EMILY [*pouting a little*]. It didn't sound at first as though he
was so anxious——

CORNELIA. No, you know—at first, he *didn't* seem to be. But
he came around. I guess it was my voice. He had to hear it
a few minutes, first. I must have impressed him. Oh, Emily,
isn't it *romantic?*

EMILY [*envious*]. Yes—very——

CORNELIA [*her dress over her arm now*]. Emily, dear—you don't mind if I take my bath first?

EMILY. No. You go ahead. I have to brush up on my colloquial French.

CORNELIA [*heading for the bathroom*]. Your what?

[CORNELIA *goes into the bathroom. There is the sound of the tub water running.* EMILY *shouts at her.*]

EMILY [*getting a slip of paper and a French grammar from her valise*]. Anywhere I saw any French words printed I copied them down. Now, I'm going to translate them. It'll make my French much more authentic—getting it directly from the natives. [*She reads from the slip of paper.*] "Ne crachez pas par terre."

CORNELIA [*from the bathroom, rehearsing*]. "The quality of mercy is not *strained*. The quality of mercy is *not* strained. It droppeth as the *gentle* rain——"

EMILY [*flipping the pages of a grammar*]. "Crachez—crachez——"

CORNELIA [*offstage, in the tub*]. "It droppeth as the gentle *rain* from heaven."

EMILY [*suddenly stopping in her translating*]. Cornelia! You know what it means? "Do not spit on the floor." [*She is dismayed.*] Oh, dear. Maybe I'd better not translate the rest of them.

CORNELIA. "It is twice blest—it blesseth him that gives and him that——" Emily! Will you bring me another twenty-five centime piece? I've run out!

EMILY [*getting up*]. Oh, sure.

CORNELIA. There should be some in my purse!

EMILY [*emptying* CORNELIA'S *purse*]. All right. I'm looking. [*She shouts back.*] No, Cornelia. There aren't any!

CORNELIA. Emily! This metre is starting to click!

[*A clicking sound is heard in the bathroom.*]

EMILY. Oh, don't worry. I must have some in mine. [*Still rather matter-of-factly, she goes to her purse and empties it out.*]

CORNELIA. Emily—hurry—please!

EMILY [*beginning to worry herself*]. Cornelia! I haven't any, either. Not a single one!

CORNELIA. Well, for heaven's sake—look in the suitcase, or someplace! I think it's beginning to smoke.

EMILY [*rushing to the valise and shaking it out*]. Oh, dear! I'll certainly try! Cornelia—*no!* We haven't got a centime anywhere. [*She runs to the bathroom door.*] Couldn't you use a franc?

CORNELIA [*terrified now*]. No, no! It wouldn't fit! Oh, Emily, what if it's going to explode?

EMILY [*becoming very excited*]. No, Cornelia! Don't get excited! Don't move! Stay right where you are. [*She runs to the door, up center.*] I'll go down the hall and borrow some!

[*EMILY dashes out, up center, leaving the door open.*]

CORNELIA. Emily! Hurry! It's going to explode! I know it!

[*We hear EMILY knocking furiously at a door down the hall, and then a door opening.*]

CORNELIA. *Emily!*

EMILY [*offstage*]. Oh, can you help me? I need a coin! Hurry.

VOICE [*offstage*]. Qu'est-ce que vous désirez?

EMILY [*agonized, offstage*]. Je veux—que—vous——[*There is a frustrated wail from EMILY and she runs back into the open doorway.*] Cornelia! What is the French word for *give?*

CORNELIA [*screaming*]. Donnez! Donnez! Donnez!

[*EMILY scoots back out.*]

EMILY [*offstage*]. Donnez-moi—vingt-cing centimes—pour le bath——Oh, never mind! There's the little girl who works here—come, come!

[EMILY *appears in the doorway, up center, dragging* THÉRÈSE *by the arm.*]

CORNELIA. Emily! What are you *doing?*

EMILY [*to* THÉRÈSE, *pointing to the bathroom*]. Could you get me twenty-five centimes, please, because my friend hasn't got any clothes on and she's going to explode!

[THÉRÈSE *screams, throws up her hands, and runs back down the hall.* EMILY *starts a few steps after her.*]

EMILY. And hurry! Hurry!

CORNELIA. Emily! It's ticking louder!

[*Suddenly, there is a loud explosion, very near. A scream from* CORNELIA *is heard.* EMILY *dashes back into the room, white.*]

EMILY. Too late. [*She covers her face with her hands, moaning.*] Cornelia—Cornelia!

[CORNELIA *rushes in from the bathroom, knotting the cord of a bathrobe.*]

CORNELIA. Emily! It exploded! But I escaped!

EMILY. Are you hurt? Are you hurt?

CORNELIA. I don't think so. I haven't looked yet.

[*There is another explosion, more distant this time.*]

EMILY. There goes somebody else's gas metre!

CORNELIA. This house is a deathtrap.

[THÉRÈSE *rushes in, up center, wild-eyed, with a Red Cross emergency kit. She barely looks at* CORNELIA, *and heads for the bathroom.*]

CORNELIA. Don't go in there! It's not safe!

[*But* THÉRÈSE *goes in.*]

EMILY. We've got to save her!

[CORNELIA *and* EMILY *rush to the bathroom door, after* THÉRÈSE. *As they get there, they stop suddenly, looking in. Their mouths drop open and their faces fall.*]

EMILY. Cornelia! There's nothing wrong with the gas metre! It's still up there. Look!

CORNELIA. Well, isn't that peculiar! Of course, I didn't actually see it blow up. When I heard the explosion, I just never looked back.

[*There is another explosion, moderately close.*]

EMILY. There it goes again!

[MADAME ELISE *rushes in, up center. She is the proprietress, Thérèse's mother. She is stout and hung with beads and at the moment out of breath from running up the stairs.*]

MADAME. What is it? What is the commotion? Where is Thérèse?

CORNELIA. Thérèse went in there. But she's all right. It didn't blow up.

EMILY. You certainly have the strangest hotel I ever heard of!

MADAME [*rushing to the bathroom and calling*]. Thérèse! Thérèse!

THÉRÈSE [*emerging from the bathroom, laughing so hard she has to hold on to the door for support*]. Maman—Maman! . . . [*She cannot speak for laughing.*]

MADAME [*shaking* THÉRÈSE]. Thérèse! Qu'y a-t-il?

THÉRÈSE [*still laughing*]. Les jeune filles! Les fêtes! [*She goes off into a new gale of laughter.*]

MADAME. Eh? Eh?

[THÉRÈSE *continues to laugh. Finally, a light dawns on* MA-DAME'S *face.*]

MADAME. Ah! Les fêtes! Ah!

[*Now,* MADAME *starts to laugh, too.* EMILY *and* CORNELIA *stare at each other and move downstage.* MADAME *sees this and comes to the table, still laughing.*]

MADAME. Mademoiselles! Pardon! Mais——[*Exuberantly, she throws out her arms.*] Happy Bastille Day!

EMILY [*puzzled*]. Well, I like that! What's she so happy about?

MADAME. The celebration! For the day of the Bastille!

CORNELIA [*dawning*]. Oh, Emily! Of course!

EMILY [*still belligerent*]. Of course, what?

CORNELIA. It's July Fourteenth. Bastille Day! They shoot off rockets, and things—like we do on the Fourth of July!

MADAME [*having pulled herself together*]. We are sorry, mademoiselles, you were frightened. It is only today, that is all. Has Thérèse made you acquainted with your room?

CORNELIA. Oh, yes. Yes. Thank you.

MADAME. The big bed here. It is historic. From a monastary it has come. It was slept in one time by—Cardinal Richelieu!

EMILY [*brightening*]. Oh, that's interesting! Who slept on the cot? Anybody?

MADAME. Only the stepbrother of my husband.

CORNELIA [*anxious to get back to her dressing*]. I'm sorry we brought you all the way upstairs, Madame Elise. I have to get dressed now. I wish we might repay you for your trouble, but——

EMILY. Wait a minute. I know! [*She dives into her valise and emerges with the safety-pockets.*] Madame Elise—would you, or Thérèse, have any use for things like this?

THÉRÈSE [*her eyes brightening up, tugging* MADAME'S *sleeve*]. Oh, Maman! Oui! Oui!

MADAME. Very well, Thérèse. If you would like them, I will accept them.

[MADAME *takes them from* EMILY *and gives them to* THÉRÈSE.]

THÉRÈSE. Merci. Thank you, mademoiselle. Merci. [*She goes to the door with the safety-pockets, fingering them lovingly.*]

MADAME [*in the doorway, going*]. Do not be afraid, mademoiselles. The explosions will go on all day, Far into the night. But tomorrow—you will be terrified at the silence!

[MADAME *goes out, up center, with* THÉRÈSE, *closing the door.*]

EMILY. Well, at least we got rid of those *things!*

CORNELIA. Look at the time I've lost! He'll be here any minute!

[CORNELIA *heads for the bathroom. There is a knock at the door.*]

CORNELIA. Emily! That's Monsieur de la Croix! Answer it while I get a dress on!

[CORNELIA *rushes into the bathroom.* EMILY *pretties herself and then goes to the door, up center, and opens it. It is* THÉRÈSE, *with the safety-pocket around her waist, and taking a telegram out of the pocket, delighted with her new carrier.*]

THÉRÈSE. A telegram has just come, mademoiselle.

EMILY. Oh! Merci!

[THÉRÈSE *bobs politely, pats her safety-pocket proudly, and goes.* EMILY *has grabbed the telegram, not bothering to close the door.*]

EMILY. Cornelia! It's a telegram. Not Monsieur de la Croix!

CORNELIA [*offstage*]. Well, open it! Open it!

EMILY [*who has been ripping it open excitedly*]. I am! My fingers get in the way! [*She reads it, her eyes popping.*] Cornelia! It's from Leo—and Dick!

CORNELIA [*practically screaming from the bathroom*]. No!

EMILY. Yes! They're in Paris! I mean they'll *be* in Paris! Tomorrow! And they want to take us to luncheon and a matinee!

CORNELIA [*thrilled, coming near the door*]. Oh, Emily—no!

EMILY. Yes, I tell you—yes! [*She melts away.*] And, Cornelia —they signed it, "Love—Leo and Dick."

CORNELIA [*coming out of the bathroom on this, in a new dress*]. Where? Where? Let me see!

EMILY. Right there! See? "Love—Leo and Dick." Isn't that ecstatic?

CORNELIA. *Isn't* it?

EMILY. Oh, Cornelia—you know what this means, though?

CORNELIA. What?

EMILY. We won't be able to start classes at the Sorbonne tomorrow.

CORNELIA [*absently, not caring too much, and lying down on the floor again for more breathing exercises*]. Oh, that's right.

EMILY. You know, Cornelia? Something that worries me?

CORNELIA [*between breaths*]. What?

EMILY [*very seriously*]. I'm afraid I'm more interested in men than in culture.

[MONSIEUR DE LA CROIX *appears in the doorway, which has been left open. At first, he is unnoticed by the girls.*]

DE LA CROIX. Pardon. Is this the room of Mademoiselle Skinner?

[EMILY *jumps.* CORNELIA, *who has been breathing loudly on the floor, emits a gasp and sits up.*]

EMILY. Oh, yes! [*She points to* CORNELIA, *on the floor.*] *That's* Miss Skinner! Won't you come in?

DE LA CROIX [*entering*]. I am Monsieur de la Croix. You were expecting me, no?

CORNELIA [*scrambling up*]. Oh, yes! Oh, Monsieur—forgive me—I was just exercising. The diaphragm, you know.

DE LA CROIX [*at his most charming*]. Then, *this* is Miss Skinner? [*He kisses her hand.*] The daughter of Otis Skinner, the so-famous American actor! I am right, yes?

EMILY. Oh, yes—that's her father!

DE LA CROIX [*greatly pleased*]. Ah! He is here, too? I may meet him? [*He looks around the room, eagerly.*]

CORNELIA. Oh, no! Father's not here. He's with Mother, in Le Havre.

DE LA CROIX [*too eagerly*]. But he is coming here—today?

EMILY. Oh, no! They're going to motor around the countryside.

DE LA CROIX. Oh, I see. . . .

EMILY. I'm Emily Kimbrough.

DE LA CROIX [*his face has fallen, disappointed; he now speaks absently, merely nodding to* EMILY]. Mademoiselle Kimbrough.

EMILY. I dance.

DE LA CROIX. But Monsieur Skinner will come to Paris—one day soon?

CORNELIA. Oh, yes, we'll all meet—eventually. Now, I intend to become an actress, Monsieur de la Croix——

DE LA CROIX. Yes. I would like very much to meet your father. Perhaps he would arrange for me some time to visit America. Surely many persons there would be happy to see me play, eh?

EMILY. Oh, I'm sure they would, Monsieur! I showed lots of girls your picture, and they were all *impressed!*

DE LA CROIX. Oh? That is good. Americans have taste, no?

CORNELIA. Now, I'm just not sure how you go *about* giving lessons, Monsieur, so if you'll just tell me——

DE LA CROIX [*resigned to the present situation, though in a pretty abstracted way*]. I see. Well! First, I will have to determine whether or not you have the necessary talent.

EMILY. Oh, she does!

CORNELIA. Emily!

DE LA CROIX [*sitting at the telephone table*]. Perhaps you could—do a scene for me, eh? That will give me some idea.

CORNELIA. Oh, yes! Of course! I have a great many prepared——

DE LA CROIX. We will take them one at a time.

CORNELIA. Well, now, let's see—there is——

DE LA CROIX. Do not stand so close. A little back, please.

[CORNELIA *moves across the room from* DE LA CROIX.]

DE LA CROIX. Yes—that is fine. Very well. You may begin. [*He sits back to listen, though not with his mind very much on it.*]

CORNELIA [*standing very erect, stiff, and nervous, clearing her throat, beginning*]. "O blessed, blessed night! I am afeared —Being in night, all this is but a dream—Too flattering sweet to be substantial."

[*In his abstraction,* DE LA CROIX *has noticed the telephone at his elbow. He interrupts.*]

DE LA CROIX. Pardon. May I please to use the telephone?
CORNELIA. Oh, of course. Go right ahead.
DE LA CROIX [*into the telephone*]. Odeon, deux-huit-quatre-six, s'il vous plaît. . . . [*He glances at* CORNELIA, *who is waiting.*] Oh, do not wait! Please continue!
CORNELIA [*swallowing, starting in again*]. "Oh, bid me leap, rather than marry Paris, from off the battlements of yonder tower; or walk in thievish ways. Or bid me lurk where serpents are; chain me with *roaring* bears!"

[CORNELIA *has gotten a little noisy on this, and* DE LA CROIX *can't hear his party.*]

DE LA CROIX [*to* CORNELIA, *with a hushing gesture*]. Please. Too much voice. It is bad for the throat. [*He speaks quickly into the telephone.*] Charles? . . . Ernest. Est-que mon costume est arrivé? . . . Vraiment? Et à propos de l'habit? . . . [*He turns to* CORNELIA, *who has subsided to a full stop.*] Go on, please. Try something with more variety. [*He speaks back into the telephone.*] Et les manchettes de dentelle? . . . Elles sont déchirées! Mais c'est impossible! [*He fumes.*]
CORNELIA [*starting in, along with* DE LA CROIX's *telephone conversation*]. "Great God! I'd rather be a Pagan, suckled in a creed outworn—So might I, standing on this pleasant

lea—Have glimpses that would make me less forlorn—Have sight of Proteus rising from the sea—Or hear old Triton blow his wreathéd horn!"

DE LA CROIX [*into the telephone, simultaneously*]. Mais je lui ai dit. La perruque doît être poudrée de nouveau—sans quoi, je ne peux pas la porter! Il faut que je paraîsse superbe avec cette perruque—c'est indispensable!

[*Meantime,* EMILY, *quite casually, is at the window, beginning to do practice ballet steps, with a hopeful eye out for* DE LA CROIX. *If ever he glances in her direction, she beams at him. He glances quickly away. At this moment, he turns again to* CORNELIA.]

DE LA CROIX. Miss Skinner. Something a little more versatile, please. A change of mood. [*He goes back to listening at the telephone.*]

CORNELIA [*with a very quick change of mood*]. "Well, Pappy, yo' sho' have cooked enuf co'n pone foah five plantations!"

[DE LA CROIX *wheels about in* CORNELIA'S *direction, startled.*]

EMILY. That's Southern dialect. Southern United States, of course.

CORNELIA [*putting her soul into it*]. "Now, all yo' li'l' pickaninnies—gathah yo'selfs around. Mammy's gwine tell y'all a stor-ry!"

DE LA CROIX [*with great dignity*]. Please! Return to the classics.

CORNELIA [*obediently, a little shaken*]. Oh, certainly—"Tell him that Electra, forsaken, braves the storm alone. She bewails away her father's fate——"

[DE LA CROIX *has turned to the telephone, but* CORNELIA *is a little loud again.*]

DE LA CROIX. Miss Skinner! Farther away, please. Yes, back! All the way back!

[CORNELIA *backs smack up against the wall.*]

DE LA CROIX. That is fine! Excellent! Now, head up. Correct posture, please!

[CORNELIA *straightens her head up until it, too, is smack against the wall and a light switch, which is located there.*]

DE LA CROIX. Splendid! Continue!

CORNELIA [*holding this rigid, flattened position*]. "Ah, memorial of him whom I loved best on earth! Ah, Orestes, whose life hath no relic save this—Now I carry thy poor dust in my hands!"

DE LA CROIX [*into the telephone, simultaneously*]. Mais, Charles! C'est extraordinaire. Il faut que les manches soient parées avec du satin!

CORNELIA [*as she continues, the lamp on the telephone table begins to flash on and off to correspond with slight movements of her head, which are her impulses to emotion in spite of the rigid position*]. "Ah, me! Ah, me! Oh, piteous dust! Alas, thou dear one, sent on a dire journey—thou has undone me——"

[DE LA CROIX *has begun to notice the flickering on and off of the light, distracting him from his telephone converation. Staring at the light, he slowly hangs up.*]

CORNELIA. "Undone me, indeed—undone me, indeed, brother mine!"

EMILY [*who has noticed it, too, and suspended her ballet exercises*]. Cornelia! What's the matter with that light?

DE LA CROIX [*getting up quickly*]. It is a short circuit. There will be a fire. I must go. [*He grabs his hat.*]

CORNELIA [*starting away from the wall*]. Ouch! [*She finds she has her hairnet tangled in the light switch on the wall.*] Emily! My hairnet's caught in this light switch!

EMILY [*running to* CORNELIA, *to help*]. Oh, *that's* what it is! You see, Monsieur, it's nothing.

[EMILY *frees* CORNELIA, *who hastily goes to* DE LA CROIX.]

CORNELIA. I have a number of other selections, Monsieur——

DE LA CROIX. No, no. It is sufficient. That will be fine, Miss Skinner.

CORNELIA [*hopefully*]. Well—what do you think?

DE LA CROIX [*considering his angle*]. Ah—I can see you have—considerable talent, mademoiselle.

CORNELIA [*thrilled*]. Oh!

DE LA CROIX. I will be happy to teach you the art of acting—for five hundred francs a lesson.

CORNELIA. Oh, that's all right!

DE LA CROIX. We will have our first lesson one week from to-day. Ah—when do you think your father will be coming to Paris, Miss Skinner?

CORNELIA. Oh, they just might pop in on us any time!

DE LA CROIX. Splendid! You have great possibilities. Well, then—[*He opens the door with a flourish.*]—next week? Same time! Eh?

CORNELIA [*seeing* DE LA CROIX *out*]. I'll be prepared, Monsieur de la Croix! I'll work like everything!

DE LA CROIX [*with a charming bow to each*]. Bonjour, mademoiselle. Bonjour.

[DE LA CROIX *puts his hat on with some dash, turns, and goes out, up center.* CORNELIA *closes the door and leans on it, starry-eyed.*]

CORNELIA. He believes in me, Emily! Did you hear?

EMILY [*she, however, is puzzled*]. Ye-es. What did you think of him?

CORNELIA [*walking across the room in a dream-state, headed for a chair*]. He's so incisive. So direct. You can tell—a master!

EMILY [*going to the cot, sitting down, frowning*]. Well, I don't know. He struck me as a little peculiar.

CORNELIA [*paying no attention, sitting back, dreamily*]. Emily
—you just don't understand about actors. All great artists are
eccentric.

EMILY [*not satisfied, but not wishing to push it*]. I see. [*She
has a new thought.*] Cornelia, I'm going to sleep on this cot.
You can have the big bed.

CORNELIA [*still staring front, happily*]. Oh, it doesn't matter,
Emily. Why?

EMILY. Well, it will help you to play character rôles.

CORNELIA [*still staring front, and rocking*]. Huh?

EMILY. Cardinal Richelieu slept in it. It'll help you to become
steeped in the culture of the past.

CORNELIA. Oh, all right.

[*There is a pause.*]

EMILY. Cornelia . . .

CORNELIA. Hm?

EMILY. Do you think he really noticed your chest tones?

[*But* CORNELIA *is lost in her happiness and doesn't even hear.*
EMILY *finally shrugs and turns to her valise.*]

CURTAIN

ACT THREE
Scene Two

SCENE: *The hotel room. The trunk has been removed and another chair has been added, down right. About eleven o'clock the next morning. It is a bright, sunshiny day and the birds are singing.*]

AT RISE OF CURTAIN: CORNELIA *and* EMILY *are still sound asleep.* CORNELIA *is in the big bed, at right, and* EMILY *on the cot, at left.* CORNELIA *snorts in her sleep, rolls over once, and seems to be scratching something. There is a moment's quiet. Then a man, the* WINDOW CLEANER, *is seen swinging into place outside the window, upstage left, humming to himself. He has some kind of belt arrangement around him to support himself at this height. He starts to apply his cleaner to the top of the window, and then stares in, noticing* EMILY *asleep on the cot. He ducks down to the lower portion of the window, which is open, and calls into the room, very good-naturedly.*]

WINDOW CLEANER. Bonjour, mademoiselles! It is already much later than early!

EMILY [*turning over sleepily*]. Huh?

WINDOW CLEANER. You should not be so late asleep on this day of enchantment!

EMILY [*propping herself up and blinking, staring at the* WINDOW CLEANER *in astonishment*]. Well! Good morning! Who are you?

WINDOW CLEANER. I clean the windows, of course. Why do you not ring for breakfast? But of course! You cannot reach the bell! [*He very conveniently reaches into the room and pulls a bell-cord hanging near the window.*]

95

EMILY [*holding the covers up around her*]. Oh! Well—thank you very much.

WINDOW CLEANER. It was nothing. But you will now not even get breakfast—[*He climbs out on his perch again.*]—you had better ask for lunch.

EMILY [*suddenly, her eyes popping*]. Lunch! What time is it?

WINDOW CLEANER [*taking out a huge watch*]. Eleven on the clock. By my father's watch, ma'm'selle.

EMILY [*shrilly, jumping out of bed*]. Eleven! Cornelia! We've overslept! [*She runs to* CORNELIA *and shakes her.*] Today's the day the boys are coming, and it's eleven o'clock!

CORNELIA [*sitting up, sleepily, and terrified*]. What? What?

EMILY [*running for the bathroom*]. We forgot to tell Thérêse what time to call us! If it hadn't been for that very kind man there! . . .

[EMILY *is out in the bathroom.*]

CORNELIA [*swinging over the side of the bed, her hair in her face*]. Man? What man? Where?

[CORNELIA *is on her feet and into the room. She sees the* WINDOW CLEANER. *He doffs his cap.*]

WINDOW CLEANER. Bonjour, ma'm'selle! I am the man who wakes up the late sleepers. Also, I clean windows. [*He goes at his work with a new vigor and complete nonchalance, humming.*]

CORNELIA [*pulling herself together, brushing the hair away from her face*]. Oh, good lord! How could we have ever let this happen?

[CORNELIA *stops in her brushing, suddenly. She begins to flex her upper lip, experimentally. Now, with the hair away from her face, we discover that the lip is swollen considerably. Slowly, staring down at it, cross-eyed, she discovers the same thing herself. She cannot believe her eyes. She dashes to her purse and takes out a mirror, staring at herself in it, with something like a mounting terror. At this point,* EMILY *returns from the bathroom, in a bathrobe, combing her hair.*]

EMILY. You can get in the bathroom now.

CORNELIA [*horror-struck*]. Emily! Look at me!

EMILY [*looking*]. Well, stop making that funny face.

CORNELIA. I'm *not* making it! Do you think I'd look like this deliberately?

EMILY. Well, how would I know? [*She runs to* CORNELIA, *looking carefully.*] Oh, it *is* like that! Cornelia! You don't think—it's a new form of the measles?

CORNELIA. Certainly not! I feel fine! But look at that upper lip!

EMILY. Yes. Just like those Ubangis in the *National Geographic.*

CORNELIA [*with a wail*]. Oh! [*She dashes to the mirror again and looks once more, meantime scratching her neck.*]

EMILY. Stop scratching yourself like that, Cornelia! You'll make something worse!

CORNELIA [*looking at her hand, surprised*]. Scratching? Was I? [*It dawns on her.*] Emily! I know what it is! That bed! [*She dashes to the bed and pulls back the hangings, staring down into it.*]

EMILY. Why, what do you mean?

CORNELIA [*slowly turning back to* EMILY]. I mean—bedbugs!

EMILY [*a screech, horrified to the soul*]. *What?*

CORNELIA. You heard what I said—bedbugs!

EMILY [*with passionate pleading*]. Cornelia, don't say that word again! Nice people don't mention such things.

CORNELIA [*furiously*]. Well, what *do* nice people say when they wake up in the morning all chewed up? And *swollen?*

EMILY. I don't think I ever *knew* a really nice person who got bitten by—who had this happen to her!

CORNELIA. Oh! You mean a bedbug can instinctively sense the presence of a *low* type?

EMILY. Oh, Cornelia, you know what I mean! I can't *believe* this has happened to you.

CORNELIA. Well, *I* can believe it! [*She kicks the bed in her anger.*] Oh, this wretched bed that Cardinal Richelieu slept in! I bet those bedbugs haven't had a bite to eat *since* Cardinal Richelieu! That's why they're so hungry!

EMILY. Now, Cornelia—you must be calm in this emergency.

CORNELIA [*suddenly more aghast than ever*]. And this is the day we're going to lunch with the boys! [*She really cries now.*] Oh, no! I won't! I'll never see them. I'd rather die. And if they ever find out the cause of my disgrace, I'll kill myself!

[*There is a knock at the door, up center, and* THÉRÈSE's *voice is heard.*]

THÉRÈSE [*offstage*]. Thèrése, mademoiselles.

[*The door opens and* THÉRÈSE *appears.*]

THÉRÈSE. Did you ring, mademoiselles?

EMILY. Why, no, we didn't, but——Oh, that's right! He did! [*She motions toward the window, but the* WINDOW CLEANER *has long since lowered himself and gone about his business.*] But he's gone.

[THÉRÈSE *looks mystified, but not for long.* CORNELIA *is bearing down on her.*]

CORNELIA. Thérèse! Would you kindly inform your mother that I found bedbugs in this bed last night. And I would like to know what she intends to do about it!

THÉRÈSE. You found the bedbugs?

CORNELIA. They found me!

THÉRÈSE [*clapping her hands together, her eyes to heaven*]. Ah! We have been trying to find them for many years!

CORNELIA. Well, the secret is out! Tell your mother this very minute!

EMILY [*trying to soothe things*]. You understand, Thérèse— we don't really blame *you*.

CORNELIA [*bitterly, striding about the room*]. No. As a matter of fact, we really blame Cardinal Richelieu!

EMILY [*easing* THÉRÈSE *out the door*]. That's all, Thérèse.

THÉRÈSE. Oui. Oui, mademoiselle.

[THÉRÈSE *scurries out, up center, and* EMILY *shuts the door.* CORNELIA *is not only pacing but scratching.*]

EMILY. Cornelia! Stop scratching your neck and your arm!

CORNELIA. But *I itch!*

[EMILY *shudders at the word.*]

EMILY [*her eyes opening suddenly*]. You know. I never really thought of it before. But just imagine how dreadful it must be to be a dog—with fleas——

CORNELIA [*desperately quiet*]. Look, Emily. If you don't mind—I have enough to worry about without imagining I'm a dog—with or without fleas!

EMILY. And the boys will be here almost any time!

CORNELIA. *What* are we going to do!

[*There is a knock on the door, up center.* CORNELIA *and* EMILY *stop, dead silent, for fear it is Leo and Dick. Then,* MRS. SKINNER'S *voice comes from outside.*]

MRS. SKINNER. Cornelia! Are you in there?

CORNELIA [*sotto voce*]. Good heavens, Emily! It's Mother!

OTIS [*offstage*]. Open up! Open up!

EMILY. And your father!

CORNELIA. What'll we do?

OTIS [*offstage*]. Stop muttering in there, and greet your parents.

EMILY. We'll just have to throw ourselves on their mercy! There isn't anything else to do. [*She runs to the door and throws it open.*]

OTIS [*as* EMILY *opens the door*]. If we won't interfere with your freedom too much!

[MRS. SKINNER *comes in.*]

MRS. SKINNER [*embracing* EMILY]. Hello, Emily, dear. [*She turns and goes to* CORNELIA.] And, baby—how are you?

OTIS [*as he charges in*]. Thought you'd like to know we were back in Paris!

[OTIS *is stopped by* MRS. SKINNER'S *scream as she recoils from* CORNELIA.]

MRS. SKINNER. Ba-by! What is it?

OTIS [*glancing, too*]. Good heavens! She's turned into an ant-eater!

MRS. SKINNER. Mercy me, child! Whatever has happened to you?

EMILY *and* CORNELIA [*together*]. Bedbugs!

MRS. SKINNER [*shocked*]. Bedbugs! Here in this room?

EMILY. Yes! Cardinal Richelieu's bedbugs!

OTIS. Of course, *that* makes it perfectly all right!

CORNELIA [*weeping, a child again*]. And, Mother! Leo and Dick—the boys we told you about—are coming any minute—to take us to lunch and the theatre—and just look at my face! Look at it! Puffed up—and shiny and blazing!

OTIS [*with appropriate gestures, to* CORNELIA'S *face*]. "It is the east—and Juliet is the sun!"

MRS. SKINNER [*sharply*]. Otis! No teasing! This is a catastrophe for a young girl! [*She leads* CORNELIA *to a chair.*] Never mind, darling. We'll get you all fixed up.

CORNELIA. But how? They're coming any time!

MRS. SKINNER. Leave that to me. Otis—run down stairs to the drugstore and get some calamine lotion—and a large bottle of disinfectant—and a pail!

OTIS [*giving a little sign of obedience and heading for the door*]. If they ask what for, I'll just tell them I'm the department of sanitation.

MRS. SKINNER. Hurry, Otis! We haven't much time!

OTIS [*in the doorway*]. Do you think we should mark this door with a big cross—as they did during the Great Plague?

MRS. SKINNER. Otis!

[OTIS *is gone, out up center.* EMILY *closes the door.*]

MRS. SKINNER. I'll start with a cold cloth. [*She crosses right.*] Is this the bathroom?

[EMILY *nods, and* MRS. SKINNER *disappears into the bathroom.*]

EMILY. Cornelia! I have an idea!

CORNELIA [*anticipating it, and screaming at her*]. If you think I'm going to put that hat with the veil on—ever again—the answer is no!

[*There is a knock on the door.* EMILY *and* CORNELIA *freeze, always afraid it is Leo and Dick.*]

EMILY. Who is it?

THÉRÈSE [*offstage*]. Thérèse, mademoiselles!

EMILY. Oh, thank heavens!

[THÉRÈSE *comes in, up center.*]

THÉRÈSE [*beginning to work down left*]. I will also dust now. Is it all right?

EMILY. Oh, sure. Sure. Go ahea——

[EMILY *glances at* THÉRÈSE *and notices with horror that she has the two safety-pockets strapped around her waist, criss-cross fashion, and is using them to carry her dustcloths, etc.*]

EMILY [*sotto voce*]. Cornelia! Look!

[CORNELIA *looks, too, and is about to let something pop out when* EMILY *closes her hand over* CORNELIA'S *mouth and gestures frantically toward the bathroom, where* MRS. SKINNER *is running water.* EMILY *shakes her head frantically.* CORNELIA *understands, and nods. They both rise and head for* THÉRÈSE.]

CORNELIA [*as they each take an arm and start to rush* THÉRÈSE *toward the door*]. Thérèse. Would you mind very much coming back a little later on? You can dust then.

[MRS. SKINNER *has just reappeared from the bathroom with a cold cloth.* CORNELIA *and* EMILY *quickly dive in front of* THÉRÈSE, *hiding her.*]

MRS. SKINNER. What's all this about not dusting now? Nonsense! Let her go right ahead. Cornelia! Come here and put this on! Emily! For heaven's sake, you'd better get dressed!

EMILY [*eager enough to get out*]. Oh, yes! That's right. I'd better.

[EMILY *slips across the back and into the bathroom, hastily.* CORNELIA *has come down to* MRS. SKINNER, *at the chair, haltingly, terrified.* THÉRÈSE, *puzzled, has gone on with her work at left stage.*]

MRS. SKINNER [*seeing the safety-pocket on* THÉRÈSE]. Well! Cornelia! Look!

CORNELIA [*gulping*]. Uh-h—what, Mother?

MRS. SKINNER. The little bags—on Thérèse. Why, aren't they just like yours?

CORNELIA. Why—they *do* seem a little similar—don't they? [*She tries to draw* MRS. SKINNER'S *attention away.*] I suppose there are lots of those in the world. They must sell them just everywhere!

MRS. SKINNER. Well, there, now! You see, I'm not the only sensible person! [*She charmingly turns back to* THÉRÈSE.] And where did you get your little bags, my dear?

CORNELIA [*before* THÉRÈSE *can open her mouth*]. Her—mother gave them to her.

THÉRÈSE [*bobbing, and smiling happily*]. Oui. Mama gave them to me.

[CORNELIA *closes her eyes with relief.*]

THÉRÈSE. And Mama was so *very* grateful when the young ladies offered them to us.

[CORNELIA *sinks, groaning.*]

MRS. SKINNER [*her lips getting firm*]. Oh, I see.

CORNELIA [*madly applying herself to the washcloth*]. Mother, help me with this cloth.

THÉRÈSE. I will come back later. I bother you now. Merci.

[THÉRÈSE *bobs and goes out, up center.*]

MRS. SKINNER [*with rising intonation*]. *Well*, Cornelia Skinner?

CORNELIA [*trying to keep herself occupied*]. Now, Mother, darling. Please don't be cross.

MRS. SKINNER [*her lips tight*]. I'm *not* cross, Cornelia Skinner!

CORNELIA. You wouldn't call me Cornelia Skinner if you weren't cross!

MRS. SKINNER. Very well, young lady. We won't discuss it. [*She starts to walk away from* CORNELIA.]

CORNELIA. Oh, Mother! Please! I wouldn't have given it to her—but—but I felt so *sorry* for the girl! All those dustcloths she has to carry around—those *heavy* cloths! And simply no place to put them—and the poor girl was burdened like a pack-horse—and besides, I just thought you meant me to wear it while traveling!

MRS. SKINNER [*sitting, unmollified, across the room, looking away*]. I see. . . .

CORNELIA. Oh, you're going to take that tone, Mother! You always *said* you wanted me to be generous!

OTIS [*kicking the door, offstage*]. Ahoy there! Open up!

[CORNELIA *flies to the door, up center, eager to get out of this conversation.*]

MRS. SKINNER. Oh, there's your father. Very well, Cornelia, we'll speak of this another time!

[MRS. SKINNER *gets up to work as* CORNELIA *admits* OTIS, *who carries a bottle of disinfectant, some lotion, and two sandwiches, wrapped in wax paper.*]

OTIS. I'm sure the clerk in that drugstore thought I was going to clean up after a murder!

MRS. SKINNER [*relieving* OTIS *of his packages*]. Now, take off your coat, dear. And maybe you'd better roll up your trousers. *You're* going to scrub! Mercy! What are these sandwiches for?

[CORNELIA *is now applying lotion.*]

OTIS. They're for *me!* I haven't had a thing since breakfast, and if the girls aren't going to lunch with *us*, I've got to have sustenance!

MRS. SKINNER [*putting the sandwiches on the telephone table*]. Not now, dear. You can have the sandwiches later—*after* you've scrubbed those bedposts!

CORNELIA [*looking at the tube of lotion*]. Mother. It says the swelling won't go down for half an hour.

MRS. SKINNER. Well, by the time you're through with luncheon, the boys won't notice a thing.

CORNELIA. But they'll see me all *through* luncheon!

MRS. SKINNER. You can keep putting a napkin to your lips, dear. Or a menu.

[OTIS *has rolled up his trousers and is pouring disinfectant into a pail.*]

CORNELIA. A napkin in one hand, and a menu in the other! How am I going to *eat?*

OTIS [*rolling up his sleeves, too*]. Let's swab the decks, Matey!

MRS. SKINNER. Now, scrub hard! They get right into the woodwork, you know.

OTIS [*with a flourish*]. Take my word for it, madame! None shall escape! It is not for nothing that I am known on two continents as Otis, the Mighty Hunter! [*He brandishes the bottle of disinfectant as he says this, and succeeds in spilling it all over himself.*]

MRS. SKINNER. Otis! Look what you've done!

CORNELIA. Father!

MRS. SKINNER. The Mighty Hunter, indeed!

OTIS [*magnificently*]. I am immersing myself in my work. [*He heaves to the bedposts, bursting out into lusty song, to the tune of "Anchors Aweigh!"*] "Bedbugs aweigh, my lads— bedbugs aweigh!"

[OTIS *scrubs vigorously. Then there is a knock at the door, up center.*]

CORNELIA. Mother! It's the boys!

LEO [*offstage*]. Hello, in there!

DICK [*offstage*]. Lafayette, we are here!

CORNELIA. Yes! Father. Quick! You'll have to hide!

[EMILY *comes dashing out of the bathroom, fully dressed.*]

EMILY. Are they here?

OTIS. And why, may I ask, do I have to hide? *I'm* a Republican!

CORNELIA. Father! Sh-h-h! Not so loud. I can't have them meet you—dripping with disinfectant!

EMILY. And we *can't* let them know about the bedbugs!

MRS. SKINNER. Mercy me, no! How indelicate!

DICK [*offstage*]. Hey! Anybody in there?

CORNELIA [*calling*]. Just a minute! [*She runs to* OTIS.] Father —please! Come in here! [*She starts him toward the bathroom.*] It'll only be for a minute—till I can get dressed! Then we're all going out—and you can meet them later!

OTIS. You don't have to pretend I'm a relative. Just say I'm the janitor.

MRS. SKINNER. Otis. You go ahead. You can help Cornelia dress.

OTIS [*being pushed into the bathroom*]. Well, at least give me my sandwiches!

[*There is a loud banging on the door by the boys.*]

EMILY [*as* CORNELIA *tugs* OTIS *into the bathroom*]. I'll slip them to you in a minute, Mr. Skinner! [*She shuts the door on* OTIS *and* CORNELIA, *and turns back into the room, smoothing down her dress.*] Are we ready?

MRS. SKINNER [*straightening her own dress*]. Yes, dear. Let them in.

[MRS. SKINNER *and* EMILY *take a second to settle themselves, composedly. Then* EMILY *goes to the door, up center, in a ladylike manner and opens it.*]

EMILY. Hello, Dick. Hello, Leo. Please come in.

DICK [*barging right in*]. Well—*finally!*

[DICK *stops as he sees* MRS. SKINNER.]

EMILY [*closing the door after* LEO *is in*]. Cornelia will be ready in a minute. This is Cornelia's *mother.* Mrs. Skinner.

DICK [*overcoming his embarrassment, as both boys go to* MRS. SKINNER, *shaking hands*]. How-do-you-do, Mrs. Skinner?

EMILY. This is Dick Winters—and Leo McEvoy, Mrs. Skinner.

MRS. SKINNER. So these are the boys who go to Dartmouth, where they have all the winter carnivals! [*She is at her most charming.*]

LEO. Yes! Well, that is—I mean, no——

DICK. We go to Harvard. We're medical students.

MRS. SKINNER. Well, now, isn't that lovely? I'm sure your mothers are very proud. It must be nice to have a medical man in the family. You get all the inside developments on science, don't you?

DICK. Yes. Yes. We do have to keep up. Say, Emily! Guess who we bumped into in London?

EMILY. Who?

LEO. Your two English friends—from the ship——

DICK. You know, "Frightfully" and "Ripping."

EMILY. Oh, them! Yes! How are they?

DICK. Harriet was fine. [*He gives her a "wise" eye.*] But Winifred was just recovering from an attack of the measles.

EMILY [*wanting to laugh, but controlling herself before* MRS. SKINNER]. No!

LEO. Yes.

DICK. You know, we just couldn't figure out *where* she caught them.

LEO. How *is* Cornelia—now—Mrs. Skinner?

MRS. SKINNER. Well, she's——Oh, she's fine, Leo! Just fine!

[DICK *has sauntered toward the big bed and is in the act of sitting on it when* EMILY *sees him.*]

EMILY. Dick! *Don't!*

DICK [*startled within an inch of his life*]. Don't what?

EMILY. Don't sit on that *bed!*

DICK [*getting off it, puzzled*]. Well—why? What's the matter with it?

EMILY. Oh—nothing—it's just that the landlady is very *fussy* about it——

MRS. SKINNER [*trying to help*]. I understand that it once belonged to Cardinal Richelieu——

EMILY. That is to say, he *slept* in it. See?

DICK [*not seeing at all, finding himself a chair*]. Well, yeah—I guess so——

[LEO *has been sniffing the air.*]

LEO. Say, what have you been using all the disinfectant for?

EMILY [*incredulously*]. Disinfectant? *Disinfectant?*

[*Suddenly,* EMILY *spots the pail where* MR. SKINNER *has left it, upstage of the big bed. She moves toward it, cautiously.*]

LEO. Yeah. This place smells like an operating room.

MRS. SKINNER. Why, I don't believe I smell anything peculiar. Do you, Emily?

EMILY [*having backed up to the window, hiding the pail behind her*]. No. Just the honeysuckle.

DICK. *Honeysuckle?*

[EMILY, *behind her back, has dropped the pail out the window, and now moves away, innocently.*]

MRS. SKINNER. I *love* France at this time of year——

[*There is a loud "Ouch" from below, outside the window.*]

LEO. Hey, what was that?

EMILY. I don't know. We keep hearing things all the time. This is the strangest old manse—I mean, pension, or something.

LEO. It sounded as if somebdoy was hurt. [*He goes to the window.*] I'd better look.

EMILY. Oh, no, you don't have to! They have a medicine kit here for emergencies.

[*But as LEO reaches the window, the WINDOW CLEANER rises from below, rubbing his head. He speaks with a patient, long-suffering tone.*]

WINDOW CLEANER. Please. If the mademoiselles will not throw things out of the windows. I have to support four children— and the two uncles of my wife. If I am injured, they will starve.

EMILY [*pacifying, and getting rid of him*]. Yes, of course. We're sorry. We'll make it up to you.

[*As the WINDOW CLEANER moves on, EMILY gets LEO away from the window.*]

LEO. But if——What are you so sorry about?

EMILY. These Gauls! You just have to humor them.

OTIS [*offstage, in the bathroom, roaring out*]. If I am not fed soon, I shall reveal all!

DICK [*jumping at the sound*]. Have you got somebody locked in there?

EMILY [*laughing it off, lightly*]. Oh, no! That's that man down the hall. He's very noisy.

DICK. Down the hall? It sounded as if it was right in there!

MRS. SKINNER. The partitions in these old hotels are so thin. So thin.

LEO. Speaking of food, I'm hungry myself. Shouldn't Cornelia
be ready?

DICK. *I'm* starved. Hey! What do you know? Sandwiches! [*He
has discovered the sandwiches on the table.*]

EMILY. Oh, my! . . .

DICK [*starting to unwrap one*]. You don't mind, Mrs. Skinner,
if we have a bite, do you?

LEO. Nothing seems to spoil our appetites.

[*LEO starts for the other sandwich. EMILY dives just in time,
snatching the other practically out of DICK'S mouth.*]

EMILY. Wait! Don't touch those!

LEO. Huh?

DICK [*startled by the grab*]. Well—hey! Why not?

EMILY [*wrapping them again and starting to back toward the
bathroom*]. Oh, they're terrible. They're not fresh. I was
going to throw them out.

DICK. That one *felt* fresh!

LEO. Emily! Are you all right?

EMILY [*at the door now, getting it open*]. It's the mayonnaise
in them. It's rancid, I think. You'd be sick. [*She slips the
sandwiches into the bathroom.*] I just *hate* rancid mayonnaise,
don't you?

DICK [*rising*]. Well, if we can't have those, let's get going.
Where's Cornelia, anyway?

LEO. Emily, you seem awfully peculiar today. Doesn't she to
you, Mrs. Skinner?

[*There is a knock on the door, up center. EMILY bounds to it.*]

EMILY. Coming!

[*EMILY opens the door, revealing MADAME ELISE, very perturbed.*]

EMILY. Yes, Madame Elise! What is it?

MADAME [*coming in, wringing her hands*]. A thousand par-
dons for not coming sooner! About the bed! What a tragedy!

DICK [*exasperated*]. What about that bed?

EMILY [*trying to get her right back out*]. Oh, Madame Elise, we've changed our minds! It doesn't matter. Everything is perfectly all right!

MADAME [*indignantly*]. It is certainly *not* perfectly all right! To think that such a thing would happen in my house! I am humiliated.

MRS. SKINNER [*coming to the rescue, and helping* EMILY *ease* MADAME *back into the hall*]. You needn't be concerned, madame. Please say nothing more about it. It was nothing.

MADAME [*staring at* EMILY *and* MRS. SKINNER]. Nothing? Mon Dieu!

EMILY. Really—it was a pleasure!

MADAME [*throwing up her hands in confusion*]. Ah! These Americans! All crazy!

[MADAME ELISE *goes out, up center, as* EMILY *quickly shuts the door.*]

EMILY. She's always apologizing because the bed isn't so comfortable.

MRS. SKINNER. Cardinals lead such *monastic* lives, you know.

DICK. Hey, look! Do we eat today, or don't we?

EMILY. Oh, Cornelia *must* be ready. Cornelia!

CORNELIA [*offstage*]. Yes, I'm coming.

DICK. Well, thank heavens!

[ALL *turn toward the bathroom door. It opens, and* CORNELIA *flits in, breezily. She has a large feather fan in one hand and is wearing a dress that more or less goes with it. She flutters the fan vividly in front of her mouth.*]

CORNELIA. Hello, everybody! Sorry to keep you waiting.

LEO. Hello, Cornelia! Gee, it's good to see you.

DICK. You're looking very well now. [*He speaks dubiously, with the fan fluttering away like that.*] I think.

EMILY. Notice the fan! Isn't it pretty? [*She gets her cape on.*]

LEO. Oh. May I see it?

[LEO *starts toward* CORNELIA. *She flits away swiftly, still fanning herself.*]

CORNELIA. Oh, you can get the *effect* much better at a distance!

EMILY. Yes! If you get up too close, it's almost ugly.

DICK. Well, look! Are we finally ready?

CORNELIA [*sweeping to the door, through and around them*]. Oh, yes! Let's not waste another minute!

EMILY. Good-bye, Mrs. Skinner!

[LEO *and* DICK *turn downstage and say good-bye to* MRS. SKINNER, *leaving* CORNELIA *free in the open doorway.*]

LEO. Yes, good-bye, Mrs. Skinner. Very pleased to have met you.

[CORNELIA *takes the opportunity, while the boys are turned away from her, to rub her shoulder vigorously against the door frame, scratching her bites.*]

DICK. Same here. Wish we could all go out together some time.

MRS. SKINNER. Yes. We must.

[DICK *turns just in time to catch* CORNELIA *in the act of scratching against the door frame.* EMILY *happens to notice her at the same instant.*]

EMILY. Cornelia!

CORNELIA [*simply slithering her arm on up the door frame, as though feeling the wood*]. Fine old doorways in this house— aren't they? [*She almost forgets to cover her mouth with the fan, and hastily brings it up again.*]

EMILY. Well, come on, boys! Don't keep us waiting!

[EMILY *and* CORNELIA *hasten out the door, up center.*]

DICK [*hastening after*]. Keep *you* waiting! Ye gods!

[EMILY *goes out, followed by* DICK *and* LEO.]

EMILY [*her voice can be heard as they go off down the hall*]. Where are we going? To the Crillon? I'd just love to go to the Crillon, but I'm so *intimidated* by headwaiters.

[MRS. SKINNER *closes the door.* OTIS *pops his head out of the bathroom.*]

OTIS. Is it legal for Otis, the leper, to come forth now?

MRS. SKINNER. Yes, they're gone, dear. Such *nice* boys! They're going to be doctors.

OTIS [*coming in, finishing the remnants of his sandwich*]. I heard what Emily said about the rancid mayonnaise. I don't think she was kidding. [*Forgetting, he sits on the bed.*]

MRS. SKINNER. I'm worried about Cornelia with that fan in front of her face. She might bump into something.

[OTIS *suddenly stops eating. He is staring front, tense. Suddenly, he slaps one leg with a resounding whack. He looks down at it.*]

MRS. SKINNER. Why, Otis! Whatever are you doing?

[OTIS *has slapped himself again. Now his eyes open wide and he remembers. He leaps away from the bed.*]

OTIS. That bed! That bed! I sat on it! [*He slaps himself vigorously and roars.*] It's man-eating! It's carnivorous! *Where's* that disinfectant?

[OTIS *is racing around the room looking for the disinfectant, with* MRS. SKINNER *jumping up to help, as the curtain falls.*]

CURTAIN

ACT THREE
Scene Three

SCENE: *The hotel room. A little more than a month later. The last day of the vacation. At center stage is a small table, with chairs above and right of it. The room now gives evidence of the packing that has been going on. Furniture is pulled about loosely and scattered packages, already wrapped, are piled here and there. The trunks have gone, and all that remain now are the two valises, which are in prominent positions, already packed, but still have their lids up for last-minute additions.*]

AT RISE OF CURTAIN: CORNELIA *and* EMILY *are both on stage. They are already dressed for the journey, even to having their hats on.* EMILY *is sitting at a table, hastily writing last-minute postcards.* CORNELIA *is pacing the floor, nervously.*]

CORNELIA. Emily, if he doesn't come, I'll die. I'll just die.

EMILY [*going on with her postcards*]. Well, Cornelia, I suspect he *won't* come.

CORNELIA [*sitting down, abruptly*]. Then, I can't go. I simply will not go back to Bryn Mawr and say Monsieur de la Croix *never* gave me a lesson!

EMILY. Well, he didn't come last week—or the week before that—or the week——

CORNELIA [*up again, pacing*]. I *know* he never came! But there were very good reasons. He had an extra performance of "The Misanthrope" one week—and he had to recite a memorial ode at the opening of that new museum another week——

EMILY [*chanting, with some sarcasm*]. And his aunt came to visit him from the Provence *last* week——

CORNELIA [*stopping, staring at* EMILY]. Emily! You don't believe it!

EMILY [*giving up her postcards for the moment*]. Oh, of course, I believe it, Cornelia. But goodness! In an hour we get on the train for Le Havre. At Le Havre we get on the boat to go home. What good would a lesson do now?

CORNELIA. What *good* would it do? It might just change my whole life, that's all! He could write to me. I could come back next summer. Why, he even might agree to become my *mentor!*

EMILY. What's a mentor?

CORNELIA. Oh, never mind!

[EMILY *resumes her work.*]

CORNELIA. And, for heaven's sakes, Emily, why are you writing all those postcards now?

EMILY. I know. Isn't it terrible the way I leave everything till the last minute!

CORNELIA. Why, we'll be home before they arrive!

EMILY. I know. But if people don't get a postcard, dated "Paris, France," they won't believe anything I tell them.

CORNELIA [*with change of tone*]. Emily—do you think I should call? Father will be here in a minute to pick us up, and I *can't* call him then!

EMILY. I don't know, Cornelia. A woman loses much of her femininity and all of her queenliness when she has to call a man.

CORNELIA [*turning strangely*]. What?

EMILY. I read that in Du Maurier.

CORNELIA [*decisively*]. Well, I don't care. I'm going to call him. [*She takes off her hat and goes to the telephone.*]

EMILY [*while writing*]. Cornelia, what did you write to Janice King about the Louvre?

CORNELIA [*the telephone in her hand*]. Why—I said it was a treasure-trove of beauty. Why?

EMILY. Because I don't want to say the same thing.

CORNELIA [*telephone in hand, threateningly*]. Emily—I'm going to do it——

EMILY [*too busy*]. What?

CORNELIA. Emily! This is the lowest ebb of my life—and there you sit writing postcards! I'm going to call Monsieur de la Croix!

EMILY [*looking up blankly*]. Oh—certainly, Cornelia. [*She goes right back to her writing, as though she had never objected at all.*]

CORNELIA. Well! I thought you were worried about my queenliness! [*She handles the telephone vigorously.*] Odeon, deux-quatre-six-un, s-il vous plaît. . . .

EMILY [*picking up another postal card*]. This one is to our maid. She *also* had bedbugs——

CORNELIA [*into the telephone*]. May I speak to Monsieur de la Croix, please? . . .

EMILY. I'd like to tell her about yours. I know she'd be interested.

CORNELIA [*aghast*]. Emily! For heaven's sakes! On a postcard!

EMILY. Oh, all right. I'll tell her about Napoleon's tomb, instead.

CORNELIA [*into the telephone*]. Hello. Monsieur de la Croix? . . . This is Cornelia Skinner. . . . Yes. Cornelia Otis Skinner. Are you going to come today and give me my lesson? . . . [*Her face falls.*] What? . . . Oh, no! You've got a matinee in half an hour? But—couldn't you come at all? . . . Oh, please, Monsieur de la Croix! Couldn't they change the bill, or something? You see, this is my last day in Paris. I'm going home. You see, my father is coming to pick us up in just a minute now, and this will be my very last chance ——[*She pauses to listen, and her expression changes.*] You *will* come? . . . Yes, that's right. My father is coming to pick us up, you see, and——Oh, Monsieur de la Croix, thank you. Thank you! [*She hangs up, glowing.*]

EMILY. Is he coming?

[EMILY *has finished her cards. She rises and is now going about the room, delicately and spiritually touching the walls and various objects belonging to the place.*]

CORNELIA. Yes! He's already in his costume, but he's going to slip into a taxi and come *right* over!

EMILY. In his costume? Oh, won't that be exciting?

CORNELIA. Isn't it *wonderful?* [*She finally notices what* EMILY *is doing.*] Emily! What are you poking at everything for?

EMILY. I'm saying good-bye to our little room.

CORNELIA. You're what?

EMILY. I'm touching everything for the last time.

CORNELIA. Well—for heaven's sake!

EMILY. I saw Norma Talmadge do it in a movie, and it was terribly tender.

CORNELIA. Oh. What movie?

EMILY. I don't remember. Except that she and the King had a love nest in the mountains, and then their four short days were over.

CORNELIA [*as* EMILY *fingers a vase*]. Well, when you say good-bye to that vase, don't drop it.

OTIS [*offstage*]. Cornelia! Open the door! Our hands are full!

CORNELIA. All right, Father!

[EMILY *runs to the door, up center, admitting* OTIS *and* MRS. SKINNER, *loaded with packages.*]

EMILY. Oh, hello, Mr. Skinner and Mrs. Skinner.

MRS. SKINNER. Hello, my dear.

CORNELIA. Good heavens! All the packages! [*She exclaims as* OTIS *unloads a particularly large one.*] What's the big one?

OTIS. *That* is the left wing of the Château Frontenac.

MRS. SKINNER. Now, Otis! It's just a board, dear.

CORNELIA. A board?

OTIS. We ripped it out of the moulding.

MRS. SKINNER. Nonsense! It was lying on the grass, where it had broken away from the terrace. I know it will make a lovely coffee tray. And so historic.

OTIS. Well, I can hardly believe my eyes, but I see you're all packed here! Therefore, let's away! Homeward!

CORNELIA. Oh, Father! You don't mean *now*—this minute?

OTIS. I most assuredly *do* mean now—this minute.

CORNELIA [*desperately, knowing her parents*]. But, Father—we have a whole hour!

MRS. SKINNER. We have to take a taxicab to the station, dear——

OTIS. And these rickety old French cabs! I'd rather go by prairie schooner! [*He starts assembling the luggage.*]

CORNELIA. But, Father! I *can't* go!

OTIS. Now, look, girl—we haven't any time for nonsense!

CORNELIA. But, I'm perfectly serious, Father!

EMILY. Oh, she *is*, Mr. Skinner.

CORNELIA [*letting it come out*]. I've got to wait for Monsieur de la Croix!

OTIS. For whom?

CORNELIA. Oh, Father, you must remember! I told you all about him.

MRS. SKINNER. That's her actor, dear.

OTIS. *Her* actor?

EMILY. From the Comédie Française!

CORNELIA. He's coming here now! He's on his way!

EMILY. *In costume!*

OTIS. Ye gods! [*He summons all his patience.*] Now, Cornelia—I hate to be in the position of discouraging your art—but we are *not* going to miss that train!

[*There is a knock on the door, up center.*]

CORNELIA. Oh, it's all right, Father! He's here!

EMILY [*who has dashed to the door and opened it*]. Oh, hello! Come in. We've been waiting!

[*It is* MONSIUER DE LA CROIX, *and he steps into the room with a flourish. He is covered with a large cape. He bows deeply to* EMILY *on entering.*]

DE LA CROIX. Mademoiselle!

EMILY [*flustered, returning the bow and the salutation*]. Mademoiselle!

[OTIS *lets out a roar of laughter.* EMILY *is hideously embarrassed and* MONSIEUR DE LA CROIX *is puzzled, as though afraid someone were making a fool of him.* CORNELIA *rushes to him, to save the day.*]

CORNELIA. Oh, monsieur! Good afternoon. This is my mother——

[MONSIEUR DE LA CROIX *bows to* MRS. SKINNER *grandly.*]

CORNELIA. ——and father——

[*This is the moment* DE LA CROIX *has been waiting for. With all his majesty, he swirls off his cloak, revealing a pretty silly-looking Seventeenth Century costume out of Molière, and approaches* OTIS.]

DE LA CROIX. Ah! Otis Skinner! Is it not? But I am enchanted to make your acquaintance! [*He gives the impression that* OTIS *is lucky to make his.*]

OTIS [*crisply, not at all pleased either by* DE LA CROIX *or by the delay*]. How-do-you-do?

DE LA CROIX [*too fulsomely*]. How much we have heard of your work in the American Theatre. In "Kismet"——magnifique!

OTIS. Thank you. Thank you. Now, my daughter here——

DE LA CROIX [*going right on, not sensing* OTIS'S *impatience*]. To speak with you is an opportunity I have long awaited!

OTIS [*glancing at his watch*]. Yes, yes. Sorry we haven't more time. [*He starts for the door.*] We'll get the trunks checked, Cornelia.

DE LA CROIX [*pursuing* OTIS, *fawning*]. It was my thought, Monsieur Skinner—that perhaps you could arrange an American tour for me. Yes?

OTIS [*in the doorway, trying to get loose*]. My dear man. You seem to be under some misapprehension. I'm an actor—not a booking agent. [*He signals hastily to* MRS. SKINNER.] Come on, Maud. We've got to find a porter. Good-bye, monsieur.

[OTIS *and* MRS. SKINNER *escape out, up center, and down the hall.*]

DE LA CROIX. But, Monsieur Skinner——

[*But* OTIS *and* MRS. SKINNER *are gone.* DE LA CROIX *is crushed. He stands in the doorway.*]

CORNELIA [*brightly, eagerly*]. Monsieur. Shall I breathe first, or do you want me to recite?

DE LA CROIX [*abstractly, irritated*]. What?

CORNELIA. I said—do you want me to——

DE LA CROIX. Oh, yes. Yes. One moment, Miss Skinner. One moment!

[DE LA CROIX *turns away from* CORNELIA, *and paces the room, chewing his lip, considering. Finally, he faces the fact that his mission has come to naught. Then he turns to* CORNELIA, *decidedly. There is a slight pause as she looks up eagerly.*]

DE LA CROIX. Miss Skinner, there is something I feel I must tell you.

CORNELIA. Oh, yes! What is it? [*She is hopeful.*]

DE LA CROIX. Well! The fact of the matter is—if we are not to mince words—to teach you would be a waste of my time.

CORNELIA. Wh-what?

DE LA CROIX. In you—I find nothing with which to work!

CORNELIA [*her mouth trembling*]. You mean——

DE LA CROIX [*letting* CORNELIA *have it, to compensate for his own failure with* OTIS]. I mean—mademoiselle—that you have no talent.

CORNELIA [*her voice breaking*]. No—talent?

DE LA CROIX [*sweeping up his cape and flinging it around him curtly*]. At least—not for acting. I would suggest you try your hand at something else. Perhaps—dressmaking?

CORNELIA [*crying aloud*]. Dressmaking?

[EMILY, *who has gradually turned to listen to the conversation, has been disbelieving, and then gradually stupefied. Now, in a rage, she can stand it no longer.* DE LA CROIX *has gone to the door and is bowing.*]

DE LA CROIX. Bonjour, mademoiselles!

EMILY [*flying to the door*]. *You*—get out of here! You get right out of here! And don't you ever show your face around here again!

[EMILY *slams the door in* DE LA CROIX'S *face.* CORNELIA *breaks into vast sobs and flings herself down at the table, her head on her arms.* EMILY *runs to her.*]

EMILY. Oh, Cornelia! Don't pay any attention to *him!* Who's he, anyway? Why—why *he* can't even speak good English!

CORNELIA [*raising her tear-stained face*]. Emily! I'm washed up! I have no talent. I'm *through!*

EMILY. Don't cry, Cornelia—don't cry.

CORNELIA [*between sobs*]. It's all right for *you* to talk! The bottom hasn't dropped out of *your* world! You have your dancing!

EMILY. Oh, my dancing isn't really any *good*, Cornelia! I just took it up to get out of gym!

CORNELIA [*paying no attention to* EMILY'S *efforts, continuing to cry*]. *Your* life is all planned—and secure! First, you'll be a great ballet dancer, and then later you'll settle down and marry! . . .

EMILY [*anything to placate her*]. No, I won't, Cornelia! I doubt if I'll *ever* marry! I doubt if anybody'll *ever ask* me!

CORNELIA [*wailing*]. Oh, yes, they will! You're just the type they *do* ask! *Everybody'll* be after you!

[MRS. SKINNER *opens the door, up center, and looks in.*]

MRS. SKINNER [*calling back*]. Yes, Otis—he's gone!

[MRS. SKINNER *comes in, up center, followed by* OTIS. MRS. SKINNER *carries a package.*]

MRS. SKINNER. And—oh, girls! I have a surprise for you!

[CORNELIA *doesn't look toward* MRS. SKINNER. *She tries to dry her eyes.* EMILY *jumps up.*]

EMILY. What is it?

MRS. SKINNER. Guess whom we found downstairs? Dick and Leo!

[LEO *and* DICK *appear in the doorway.*]

MRS. SKINNER. They've come to see you off.

LEO. Yes. Can we be any help?

DICK. Hi—Emily!

[DICK *goes to* EMILY, *taking her hand.*]

MRS. SKINNER. Well, Cornelia! Aren't you glad to see the boys?

[CORNELIA *turns her head farther away.*]

MRS. SKINNER. Cornelia! What's the matter with you?

EMILY. Oh, Mrs. Skinner! It's Monsieur de la Croix!

[OTIS *raises an eyebrow.*]

CORNELIA [*finally turning toward them, impulsively, no matter what her tear-stained face may look like*]. Mother! He said I had no talent! [*Her voice breaks again and she is off, into fresh sobs.*]

MRS. SKINNER. Baby!

OTIS [*angrily*]. Oh, he did, did he?

EMILY [*bitterly*]. He said she should study dressmaking.

CORNELIA. Yes! [*There are more wails.*]

OTIS. Why, the little—chipmunk!

MRS. SKINNER. That's right, dear—chipmunk!

CORNELIA [*going away from them, shaking her head as she cries*]. My life is over! . . .

MRS. SKINNER. Now, you're not going to pay attention to anything *he* said!

LEO [*ready for action*]. Say, who is this guy, anyway?

OTIS. Just a cheap opportunist. What does he know about acting?

CORNELIA [*abandoning herself*]. No—no, he's right. Don't try to comfort me. I'll never act. And after all the time I wasted on my diaphragm!

MRS. SKINNER. Cornelia! And here I brought you another surprise, too! A present—for both of you! [*She unwraps the package under her arm.*]

LEO. Cheer up, Cornelia! *We* believe in you!

EMILY. What's the present, Mrs. Skinner?

[MRS. SKINNER *unwraps two brand new safety-pockets.*]

EMILY. Oh, mercy! [*She runs to* CORNELIA, *keeping her eyes turned away.*] You don't want to see them, Cornelia. Not in your state of mind!

MRS. SKINNER. I brought them to show you all is forgiven, dear. See?

OTIS. Cornelia! Pull yourself together.

CORNELIA [*wiping away the tears, dramatically*]. Yes, Father. I will. It's all over now. I won't be in the theatre. [*She speaks bitterly.*] I'll just lead a drab, dreary, bourgeois life. Just a cog in the wheel. I'll do office work. Probably for an insurance man.

MRS. SKINNER. But, baby——

CORNELIA [*working herself up now*]. I can just see myself. Into the office bright and early at a quarter to nine. [*Unconsciously, she starts to act this all out for them in her bitterness.*] "A fresh flower for your desk, Mr. Heffelswinger. Oh, yes, Mr. Heffelswinger. I *did* make carbons of that invoice. *Yes,* sir! It's filed under "Z" in second year premiums. Shall I look it up for you, Mr. Hesselfinger, or whatever your name is! What? You say we sold two new policies today? *Sidewalk* insurance? My goodness, that is exciting, Mr. Fesselslinger!"

[*The* WINDOW CLEANER *has come up to the window, beginning to wash it, and stops to listen, as* CORNELIA, *filled with furious and bitter energy, goes on acting.*]

CORNELIA. That's how it'll be! I'll stay there for years—and then finally I'll marry Mr. Heffelswinger. And the only time I'll speak in public is to the neighbors over the back fence! [*She moves about, mimicking.*] "Yes, my George says I make the best spoonbread he ever tasted! How do I make it? Well, I take my bowl, and I break my two eggs into it. Then I add my flour and mix it all together. Did you do much canning this year? Oh, yes—yes, I did. Sixteen cans of peaches, and fourteen tomatoes. I've decided to make *dark* fruitcake this Christmas. George likes it better than light fruitcake. *No!* Is that so! My dear, I haven't read a newspaper all week—I've been so busy cleaning out my downstairs closets. That's *right*—that's what I always say. There's nothing gives you a feeling of real satisfaction like hanging out a nice, snowy wash!"

[*The* OTHERS *have at first made gestures of protestation and consolation, but* CORNELIA'S *energy has subdued them. Gradually, they have dropped into chairs, listening.* OTIS *listens quite keenly, after a while.*]

CORNELIA. The most glamorous thing *I'll* ever do will be to stand out on the porch Sundays, watching the men pitch horseshoes! "Good for you, George! Good for you! Don't let Lem get all the ringers! I expect to go with you to the county tournament!" And then we'll be old—sitting on that darn front porch—rocking and rocking—and talking over our *thrilling* life together! [*She flops into a chair, rocking back and forth with malignant fury.*] "Yes, George. Yes, George. *Yes*, George! It's been—*wonderful!*" [*This last is practically*

a scream, and it rides off into near tears and sobs as her en-
ergy exhausts itself and she huddles in the chair, crying.]

[*There is a moment of silence from them* ALL. *Then the* WIN-
DOW CLEANER *breaks into furious applause.*]

WINDOW CLEANER. Bravo! Bravo!

[ALL, *startled, turn toward the* WINDOW CLEANER, *and then*
turn to stare at CORNELIA.]

LEO. Say, Cornelia! That was better than Lady Macbeth!

DICK. You know, it *was*.

EMILY. Cornelia! You had me all taken up in it!

WINDOW CLEANER [*with a gesture*]. Magnifique! Magnifique!
   [*He goes on about his business, and in a moment disap-*
   pears.]

CORNELIA [*vaguely, coming out of it*]. Huh?

LEO. Gee, Cornelia! You're a whole show in yourself.

EMILY. Cornelia—when we get back to school, you've got to do
   that for the girls!

LEO. Say, Cornelia—when you come to the prom—at Thanksgiving—would you do it then?

EMILY. Cornelia! Could you do something like that in the theatre?

CORNELIA. Oh, no!

MRS. SKINNER. Why, I believe there *is* something like that! I've
   seen it done. What do they call it, Otis?

OTIS [*quietly, still staring at* CORNELIA]. Monologue.

MRS. SKINNER. That's right! Monologues!

CORNELIA. Oh, don't be silly! I couldn't just act all by myself! . . .

MRS. SKINNER. The people *I* saw do it got *paid* for it.

CORNELIA. Mother—you don't mean—you think people would
   pay *money*—for that?

EMILY. I would. Cornelia!

CORNELIA. Oh, Emily! But——

OTIS [*quietly*]. Cornelia. . . . There might be something in it.

CORNELIA [*overcome*]. Father!

OTIS. What you did just now was—quite good. I'd think about it.

CORNELIA [*completely flustered in her sudden happiness*]. Well —well—now—for heaven's sake! Well, gee! Then I'm glad I *did* work on my diaphragm!

[ALL *laugh, releasing the mood.* OTIS *suddenly looks at his watch.*]

OTIS. Ye, gods! Now if you'll get to work on your face—so we can get out of here! . . .

CORNELIA [*remembering her tear-stained appearance*]. Oh, my goodness!

[CORNELIA *runs for her vanity, as* ALL *leap up and get busy.*]

OTIS. *We'll miss that train!*

MRS. SKINNER [*gathering up her own bundles, with* OTIS'S *help*]. Everything's packed, isn't it?

EMILY. Yes! I just have to close them!

[EMILY *locks* CORNELIA'S *valise and starts for her own.*]

DICK. We'll take them down for you.

OTIS. Fine, boys, fine! I'll go line up a taxi.

[OTIS *staggers out, up center, with an armload of* MRS. SKIN- NER'S *bundles.* MRS. SKINNER, *also loaded, scurries out after him.*]

MRS. SKINNER. Otis! Otis! We've got my board, haven't we?

[OTIS *and* MRS. SKINNER *disappear down the hallway.* DICK *comes to* EMILY *as* LEO *starts toward* CORNELIA, *who is des- perately repairing her face.*]

DICK. I wish we were going all the way home with you, instead of just to the boat.

LEO. Cornelia—remember you said you'd write.

CORNELIA. If you write first.

LEO. Oh, I will! Which bag is yours—so I can carry it?

EMILY. That's hers. And, Dick, this is——Oh, wait a minute!

[EMILY *has been in the act of shutting her own valise. Now, she opens it full again, takes out the safety-pockets which Mrs. Skinner has placed there, and quickly, but stealthily, slips them under the cot. Then she returns and shuts her bag.*]

EMILY. All right. And hurry on down, now! Give Mr. Skinner the impression that we're coming!

DICK [*taking the valise, but putting it down for a moment and moving toward* EMILY]. Child, draw closer.

EMILY. Huh?

DICK [*putting his hands on her shoulders*]. I'm going to do this simply because I don't want you to have any misconception of my true nature.

EMILY. Huh?

DICK. I'd never want you to think I was backward.

[DICK *kisses* EMILY *in an efficient manner, and then releases her. She turns front.*]

EMILY [*with a triumphant sigh*]. Engulfed!

DICK [*to* LEO, *who is mooning at* CORNELIA]. Come on, boy. Snap into it!

[LEO *grabs up* CORNELIA'S *valise as* DICK *takes* EMILY'S *and they go out, up center, and down the hall.*]

CORNELIA [*finishing the make-up job*]. There! I look halfway human again.

EMILY. I really made them go ahead, Cornelia—so we'd have the last moment—together.

CORNELIA [*turning to* EMILY *slowly*]. That's right. It's all over, isn't it?

EMILY. Yes.

CORNELIA [*as they look at each other for a moment, then impulsively going to* EMILY]. Come on, now!

[EMILY *and* CORNELIA *go to the door, up center. In the door-way,* CORNELIA *turns to* EMILY.]

CORNELIA. Oh, Emily! We're going!

EMILY. Such a lovely, lovely summer—and it's all over.

CORNELIA [*nodding, feeling it, too*]. Yes. [*She speaks hopefully.*] Of course, we may come back again.

EMILY. But even if we do, Cornelia—it won't be the same. We won't be together. And we won't be nineteen, Cornelia. Not ever again.

CORNELIA [*slowly*]. No. . . . [*She turns to look back at their room.*]

[EMILY *turns back, too. They stare at it a moment. Then* CORNELIA *speaks to the room.*]

CORNELIA. Good-bye.

EMILY [*to the room*]. Good-bye.

[*With a catch in their throats, they turn quickly and go out down the hall. Immediately,* MADAME ELISE *and* THÉRÈSE *enter, looking back down the hall, as though they'd just passed the girls.* MADAME ELISE *comes in brusquely and, with great efficiency, begins to rip the sheets off the big bed.* THÉRÈSE *sees something. She stoops down quickly, and gasps.* MADAME ELISE *turns to see what it is.* THÉRÈSE *rises, the new safety-pockets dangling in her hand. She turns and starts madly out the door, after* EMILY *and* CORNELIA, *with the safety-pockets.*]

THÉRÈSE. Mademoiselle Skinner! Mademoiselle Kimbrough! Mademoiselle Skinner! Mademoiselle Kimbrough!

[THÉRÈSE *is running down the hall as the curtain falls.*]

CURTAIN

Production Notes

COSTUME SUGGESTIONS

GENERAL: The costumes are of the period of 1923. Women's dresses were of the long-waisted, shapeless style, clearing the ground by about ten inches. Hats were deep-crowned and of fairly wide brim with trimming of feathers for the younger miss and often brimless for the matron. Suits of gabardine or tweed had three-quarter length coats or capes with shirtwaist blouses. Afternoon dresses were of pastel or bright colors in tailored georgette; late afternoon dresses were of flowered chiffon. Evening dresses were sleeveless, sometimes of uneven hemline, and a trifle longer than daytime dresses. They were made of satins, or of heavy crêpe or georgette, often richly beaded.

Men's suits were made of lightweight materials in gray, light brown, powder blue, tan, or white, usually single-breasted. Top-coats were of lightweight tweed. Hats were of soft felt. For formal afternoon wear the striped trousers, spats, and cutaway coats were in style, with black soft felt hats. For evening wear the young men wore tuxedos and wing collars.

The suggestions which follow are based on the costumes worn in the tryout production at The Catholic University of America, Washington, D.C.

CORNELIA: She appears in the first scene in a blue gabardine suit and black felt hat. The suit will have to be a two-piece outfit, so her mother can tuck the safety-pocket down into the skirt. She next appears in a black satin evening gown and multi-colored velvet scarf. At the opening of the second act she is in a bright-colored evening dress of cut velvet. The nightgowns the girls wear are white muslin, long-sleeved, and high-necked, and floor length with ruffled hem. The bathrobes are of silk or satin. At the opening of the third act Cornelia is in a blue-flowered chiffon. For her meeting with Monsieur de la Croix she changes quickly to a green beaded evening dress. For luncheon with the boys she wears a long-sleeved red crêpe afternoon dress. She appears in the last scene in her blue traveling suit.

EMILY: She appears in the first scene wearing a blue checked suit with cape. Her evening dress in the second act is of pink satin with uneven hemline. Her dress for leaving the ship is a tailored flowered silk, in which she appears again at the opening of the third act. For luncheon with the boys she wears a tailored georgette. Her traveling suit in the last scene is of rust-colored gabardine or tailored tweed. Her nightgown and bathrobe are similar to Cornelia's.

MRS. SKINNER: She wears a dark purple suit and brimless deep-crowned hat in the first act. For her appearance at the beginning of the third act she wears a dark blue dress with bright trim. At the end of the third act she is wearing a pin-stripe black velvet suit.

OTIS: He appears in the first act in a powder blue suit, light tweed topcoat, and a soft felt hat. At the beginning of the third act he is wearing formal afternoon attire of striped trousers, spats, dark cutaway coat, and black felt hat, and at the end of the act he appears again in the powder blue suit.

LEO *and* DICK: They change their suits often. Leo is wearing a dressing gown in the first act. In the second act the boys appear in tuxedos and wing collars. When they leave the ship they are wearing light colored suits. They change their suits for their entrance in the third act and again for the closing scene of the third act. Blazers are suitable for shipboard use.

STEWARD: He wears a white uniform, choker collar, and cap.

STEWARDESS: She appears in a bright blue uniform dress with white collar, cuffs, apron, and headpiece.

ADMIRAL: He wears a dark blue uniform with gold braid, gold buttons, and a cap.

PURSER: He wears a standard Purser's uniform and cap.

ENGLISH GIRLS: They appear in trim tweed suits with shirt-waist blouses.

129

INSPECTOR: She wears a dark blue uniform and cap with high-button shoes.

DE LA CROIX: He appears the first time wearing striped trousers, spats, a Prince Albert coat, and wing collar. For his last appearance he wears a velvet Seventeenth Century tunic and a dark sweeping cape.

MADAME ELISE: She wears a black tailored dress and high-button shoes. She also has many strings of beads about her neck.

WINDOW CLEANER: He appears in dark trousers and a loose shirt and cap.

THÉRÈSE: She wears a flowered dress and apron—very trim.

CHARACTER NOTES

CORNELIA is a tall, handsome, vital girl. When she is not acting out a little scene for herself, she is direct and very down to earth. She sometimes makes rather rapid transitions between these two. Everything about her personality is colorful and alive.

EMILY is a delicately pretty girl. She is conservative rather than shy, and never flamboyant in the way that Cornelia sometimes is. She is rather naive, but not in the standard, wide-eyed manner; rather, she repeats absurdities in a calm, matter-of-fact fashion, so that you can see that everything she says, no matter how wild, is perfectly logical to her.

LEO is a straightforward, earnest youth, who would probably be classed as an "eager-beaver" by his friends. He is always sincere, serious, and likeable.

DICK might be called a "wise guy," except that he is not at all offensive about it. In fact, his sophistication is easy, charming, offhand. He is always two jumps ahead of Leo, toward whom his manner is almost fatherly.

OTIS SKINNER is expansive in a slightly theatrical way, though always dignified. He is a witty man, and, if his remarks are sometimes a little caustic, they always stem from a great good humor. He is both colorful and impressive.

MRS. SKINNER is exquisitely refined, and rather conservative in effect. Her manner is gracious, and if her remarks sometimes seem a little disorganized, the effect is one of charming vagueness, perfectly cultivated, and never the stock dizzy female.

MONSIEUR DE LA CROIX is showy and overdramatic, in an elegant way. His weariness with Cornelia's recitations is perfectly obvious—he is bored to death—and his joy at finally meeting Otis is even more obvious, perhaps vulgar. He is ham—pure and simple—but with a relish.

WINIFRED *and* HARRIET are crisp, breezy, matter-of-fact, and hardly aware of the other people past whom they breeze. When they become aware of them, they are very cheery.

THE STEWARD is a hard-working little man who doesn't understand young girls, and finds them far too much for him. His bewilderment increases with the first act, until he is almost in tears.

THE PURSER is a crisp, businesslike man with a poker face. He is so used to barking orders and handling complaints with authority, that he never betrays what he is thinking. As a result, when he comes to reward Emily at the end of Act One, it is impossible to tell from his manner, and his quick anger with Leo and the Steward, that he has really come on an errand of congratulation. This last is important, since suspense must be maintained until he makes his final announcement.

THE ADMIRAL is a florid, overly-gracious, professionally charming man. It is his business to make a good impression on the passengers, which he does. His manner is most ingratiating.

THE WINDOW CLEANER is easy, friendly, and talkative. He does not seem intrusive or like a busybody when he rings the bell for Emily, or joins the conversation in the last scene, because he is habitually intimate with everybody, simply accepting their confidence as his due. As a result, he is very shocked and hurt when he is hit on the head, and extremely patient and dignified when he remonstrates with Emily about the matter.

THÉRÈSE is pretty and doll-like.

MADAME ELISE is efficient and garrulous.

THE STEWARDESS is grim and businesslike.

THE INSPECTOR is super-efficient, brusque, and sharp-eyed.

PROPERTY PLOT

ACT ONE

GENERAL: Bunks, small table with rose in a vase, chaise lounge, hassock, service tray with dishes on it, life preserver.

CORNELIA: Purse containing two tags for trunks, coin, currency, passport, papers; valise containing articles of clothing, earrings, long handkerchief, nightdress, bathrobe, black dress, and one other dress.

EMILY: Purse containing tags for trunks, passports; valise containing dress, articles of clothing, nightdress, bathrobe; dress on hanger, basket of fruit, safety-pocket.

MRS. SKINNER: Purse, and package containing safety-pocket; gloves; watch.

OTIS: Two sets of wrapped packages, among them are a hatbox, suitbox, etc., and Emily's purse.

STEWARD: Cap, five trunks, and Cornelia's valise.

DICK: Suitcase.

PURSER: Safety-pocket.

ADMIRAL: Two safety-pockets in brief case.

HARRIET: Toothbrush, glass.

WINIFRED: Toothbrush and paste.

ACT TWO, *Scene One*

GENERAL: Same as Act One—valises on lower bunk, change of flowers, add chair left of up center door.

CORNELIA: Comb, nightdress, bathrobe.

EMILY: Nail buff.

ACT TWO, *Scene Two*

GENERAL: Same as Act One.

CORNELIA: Mirror, vanity case, lipstick, white powder, large coat, hat with veil.

132

EMILY: Combs, wrapped piece of chocolate cake.
DICK: Glass and bottle of medicine.
ADMIRAL: Loving cup in brief case.
MATRON: Pad and pencil.
WINIFRED: Toothbrush.
HARRIET: Glass.

ACT THREE, *Scene One*

GENERAL: Cot, French bed, trunk, armchair, straight chair, pictures, telephone table and French phone, lamp on table.

CORNELIA: Valise containing dress, bathrobe; purse containing slip of paper, mirror, money; hairnet.

EMILY: Valise containing safety-pockets, dresses, nightdress; purse containing letters, money (on the telephone table at the end of scene); French book.

THÉRÈSE: Telegram, safety-pockets (given her by Emily), first aid kit.

ACT THREE, *Scene Two*

GENERAL: Same as Act One, except for the trunk, which is removed, chair added, down right.

CORNELIA: Purse with mirror on telephone table, comb on chair near bed, French fan, bathrobe. NOTE: Her swollen lip in this scene can be managed very simply by chewing up three or four sticks of chewing gum and inserting them above the teeth.

EMILY: Bathrobe, bedroom slippers.

MRS. SKINNER: Washcloth.

OTIS: One bottle of disinfectant, one bottle of lotion, two wrapped sandwiches, cloths, brush, pail.

THÉRÈSE: Five dustcloths in safety-pockets.

WINDOW CLEANER: Belt, cloth, large watch.

ACT THREE, *Scene Three*

GENERAL: Table and two chairs, papers strewn around, postcards, pen and ink on table.

CORNELIA: Hat, valise, packages, vanity case.

EMILY: Postcards, French book in valise, papers.

MRS. SKINNER: Two safety-pockets, wrapped, and other packages.

OTIS: One large package.

INSTRUCTIONS FOR MAKING SAFETY-POCKETS

Two tan and two yellow leatherette pockets are needed. Fold a piece of material—8¾″ x 20½″—into three parts, pointed at one end, as indicated in diagram. Before stitching either side, insert a one-inch strap into a slit about one-quarter of an inch from the edge. The straps should be long enough to go around the waists of the characters and touch the knees. The strap should have a snap or buckle to fasten around the waist, so that the pocket will hang directly to the knees.

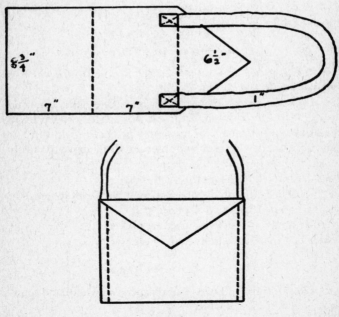

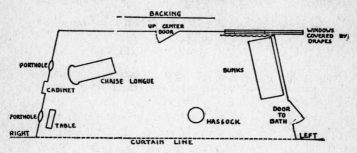

The cabin of a ship.

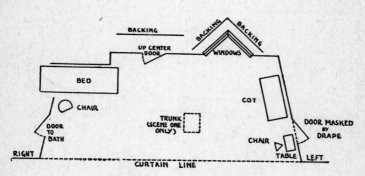

The hotel room in Paris.

Directors write us about

OUR HEARTS WERE YOUNG AND GAY

"The board of education voted to record in their minutes a permanent note of congratulation to the cast and director."
—Johanna Cramer, High School, Paxton, Ill.

"The cast got a big 'boot' out of studying the actions and customs of the early twenties."—Emily L. Mitchell, High School, Revere, Mass.

"We find it even better in modern costume than in 1920 costume, as suggested."—A. F. Gerwig, Elmhurst High School, Ft. Wayne, Ind.

"The town is still talking about it—nearly three months later. The enthusiasm was so great that a group wished to start a Little Theatre movement and one is now under way."—Ruth K. Tate, Haverling Central School, Bath, N. Y.

"It was 'alive' with sparkle and 'ginger' to amuse students and adults alike."—Mrs. Leland Jensen High School, Gallup, N. M.

"More laughs than any play given."—Sylvia Furlong, Miami Senior High School, Miami, Fla.

"The audience was charmed also by the warm delightful comedy and the clean, wholesome fun."—Joyce Hammontree, Cohn High School, Nashville, Tenn.

"Everyone liked the play. It was so sparkling and joyous— as well as humorous—the unexpected type."—Sister Rose, St. Mary Academy, Nauvoo, Ill.

"I thought the play as literature and theatre was a superior one."—Howard W. Miller, High School, Catonsville, Md.

"Each character was distinctive. Each had 'the limelight' for a time, and the young people appreciated that."—Lois B. Clipner, River Falls, Wis.

"The 'twenties' sold the play—and the human characterizations touched the hardest hearts. A nostalgic treat to the parents and a picnic for the younger generation."—Marcelline McDermott, High School, Los Gatos, Calif.